KEVIN SHEEDY'S BOMBER JACKET

Biz Help - www.cciwa.com

Glen Humphries

KEVIN SHEEDY'S BOMBER JACKET

AUSTRALIAN FOOTBALL'S CONTROVERSIES AND CURIOSITIES

GELDING STREET PRESS

A Gelding Street Press book
An imprint of Rockpool Publishing Pty Ltd

PO Box 252
Summer Hill
NSW 2130 Australia

geldingstreetpress.com
Follow us! geldingstreet_press

Published in 2025 by Gelding Street Press

ISBN: 9781922662200

Design and typesetting by Christine Armstrong, Rockpool Publishing
Edited by Lisa Macken

A catalogue record for this book is available from the National Library of Australia

Printed and bound in China
10 9 8 7 6 5 4 3 2 1

THIS BOOK IS DEDICATED TO THE MIGHTY PORT KEMBLA BLACKS. AND OTHER PARK FOOTY PLAYERS EVERYWHERE.

CONTENTS

‘OF COURSE IT’S A GRUDGE MATCH,’ SHEEDY SAID. ‘WHY WOULDN’T IT BE?’

INTRODUCTION

Items of clothing are not supposed to start a sporting rivalry. Geographical proximity will do that, as will the loss of a grand final in the past, and a player bad-mouthing his old team as he joins a new one: that will do it too. The betrayal of a much-loved player viewed as a son to many who decides to go somewhere else will spark up a rivalry, as will both teams being high-flyers and the success of one requiring the failure of the other . . .

. . . but a jacket? That's not meant to inspire any sort of animosity, a key ingredient in sporting rivalry, yet that's what happened shortly after the full-time siren at the Melbourne Cricket Ground (MCG) on the afternoon of 18 July 1993. It was the round 18 clash between the Essendon Bombers and the West Coast Eagles, a game that put the two coaches – Kevin Sheedy and Mick Malthouse – head to head. They had been team-mates at Richmond in the 1970s, which can be enough to spark a coaching rivalry. It's always a little bit sweeter when a victory includes beating a former team-mate.

There was plenty riding on this game. With the finals a month and a half away, it was a battle for the last spot in the top six. West Coast had it, while the Bombers were right behind them in seventh place. That Essendon were so close so late in the season was a surprise, because in 1993 the team was blooding a bunch of kids. The media called them the 'Baby Bombers'. That season was supposed to be an investment in the future: give them a taste of top-level footy and see which players rose to the occasion.

They pretty much all did. What was supposed to be a rebuilding year started to promise more as the kids got in sync and managed to sneak into the top six by round 10. They stayed there until the week before the West Coast match, when North Melbourne whomped them by 38 points. The Eagles, on the other hand, were the defending premiers. They'd been a fixture of the top six from the start of the season but were coming off a bye in round 15, so they needed to get a win to keep the momentum going into the finals.

The Eagles took charge early, taking a 14-point lead into quarter-time and 11 points at the half, but it was clear the Baby Bombers weren't going away. The kids pounced in the third quarter to lead by 13 points, then the Eagles came back in the last quarter to lead by four with less than a minute on the clock. The ball went to Bombers' big man Paul Salmon inside the 50, who was awarded a free kick for a push in the back from defender Glen Jakovich. There wasn't a lot of confidence in the Big Fish that afternoon: he'd only kicked three behinds. Salmon remembered team-mates saying it would be in his best interests to put it between the big sticks. 'That was just an indication of the tension in the game,' Salmon told the *Sunday Age*. 'I laid back on it more than I'd like. There was an initial flutter of the heart and I thought "Oh, god", but actually from hand to boot it was good.'

It was good after that point too: the goal gave Essendon the win, although Salmon's reaction after kicking six seems to speak more about relief and thinking about what may have happened if he missed rather than any jubilation. Around 40 seconds later the siren sounded, which is about when Sheedy and his jacket made an appearance. In the Essendon coaches' box, just like on the field, there were plenty of hugs, then Sheedy left the box and started walking down the stairs to the field. He was carrying his club jacket in his left hand and, overcome by the moment, he raised it over his head and waved it in the air in celebration.

'I got a little bit excited that day,' Sheedy remembered in the *Herald Sun* in 2020. 'I just walked out and did it without even thinking. It was an unbelievable win. West Coast had won the flag the year before and we were a team that sort of came from nowhere.'

As Sheedy lowered his jacket he had a quick glance over his left shoulder, which some people have suggested was in the direction of the Eagles' coaches' box to make sure Malthouse saw it. The Eagles coach did, according to a West Coast official, and it wasn't the only thing that had Malthouse riled up. After the match he pulled out the expletives to describe the umpiring performance and also backed a footy journalist into a wall.

The win saw Essendon back in the top six, and they finished the season on top. West Coast was there too at the end of the regular season, though only just: they'd squeaked into sixth spot ahead of the Cats on percentages. West Coast won their elimination final while Essendon went down by two points to Carlton, which set up a semi-final meeting between the two teams that helped to solidify the rivalry. The Bombers won by 32 points and won the flag two weeks later. In that match against

West Coast the waving of clothing over the head resurfaced, though this time it was the Essendon fans doing it.

From that point on it became a tradition after West Coast–Essendon matches for the winning fans to wave jackets, scarves or whatever was close to hand. When the premiers visited Subiaco in the back end of the 1994 season, the Eagles won 11.14 (80) to 5.14 (44) over a very inaccurate Bombers outfit. As Sheedy left the ground, fans joyfully raised various items over their heads and gave them a wave. The reaction gave lie to Malthouse's claims in *The Age* just days before the match that 'It's not a grudge match for us on Sunday, it's the same as any other game.'

Even in 2001 the Eagles tried to hose down any talk of grudge matches, which Sheedy just rubbished. 'Of course it's a grudge match,' he told the *Sunday Times*. 'Why wouldn't it be? It started with that jacket-twirling thing at the MCG and last year I got fined for that half-time incident.'

What Sheedy called an 'incident' saw him fined $7,500 for making a throat-slitting gesture towards Eagles forward Mitchell White. Assistant coach Mark Harvey later said that after seeing Bombers' replacement Mark Johnson lying on the turf, he told Sheedy that White did it and the coach should have a spray at the Eagles player at half-time. Instead of a spray, Sheedy chose a throat-slitting gesture.

Despite that jacket sparking a Bombers–Eagles rivalry, Sheedy later felt less than proud of it. 'It was something you never did,' he said on *Talking Footy* in 2020. 'I mean, I've gone out and head-butted blokes and belted blokes and I've got no problem with all of that, but to wave your jacket and just get remembered for that, that's a problem.' Perhaps the core of the problem lies in the mother-son relationship. After the 1993 match Irene gave her son a call. 'I thought Mum was ringing to congratulate me on the win,' Sheedy later explained. 'Instead she said, "Kevin, I'd just like to remind you that there's an idiot born every day."'

The rich history of Australian rules is chock full of stories like Sheedy and his jacket, even before the modern-day wall-to-wall coverage the sport now attracts. Some of them you'll read about in the following pages, including tales about the player who allegedly took the field with a hook where his arm should have been, a Carlton hard man who tarnished his legacy somewhat by mistakenly thinking he was an actor and a candidate for the worst team of all time.

Sure, there are stories you already know, which is inevitable given the respect footy shows for its own history. They include Dogs coach Luke Beveridge's actions on the dais after the 2016 grand final and Tayla Harris taking on the tools that live online, but there are also a few moments that live in the margins such as the shortest coaching stint in league history, footy players in court for punching on during a match and why Fitzroy fans in the early 1900s were terrible.

In the pages that follow you might find something you didn't know about the great game of Australian rules. You'll surely be reminded of some of the iconic and infamous moments from more than a century of the code.

REALLY, WHAT WERE THE OFFICIALS THINKING BY ALLOWING SOMEONE WITH A *HOOK* TO PLAY FOOTBALL?

—

1

OUT COMES THE HOOK

Okay, so let's say there was a one-armed Australian rules player running around in the late 1800s. It seems a safe bet that sports writers might mention that in their reporting from time to time, because it's not as though the late 1800s were a wonderfully enlightened time. It was an era when phrases such as 'cripple' and worse were used without a second thought. Now, if that player took the field with a hook in place of the missing limb it would be a *certainty* that it would be mentioned in newspaper coverage, especially if that aforementioned hook took someone's eye out or inflicted some other serious injury. Really, what were the officials thinking by allowing someone with a *hook* to play football?

This player supposedly sporting a hook was one Alex Bruce, though some online pundits insist it was George Bruce. That can be easily disproved by looking at photos of Georgie Boy, which clearly show him with not one but two arms. So, okay, not George Bruce, but is it Alex Bruce who is the one-armed man? Cue the shoulder shrugs.

The main source of the story of one-armed Bruce and his hook comes from the memoirs of Victorian Football Association president T.S. Marshall, written in 1896, more than a decade after Bruce played. 'He had one arm, but his one arm was equal to most people's two backed up as it was by an artificial one with an iron hook at the end of it,' Marshall wrote. 'He was a good tempered and fine player, but I verily believe he was the cause of more oh's and ah's . . . than a dozen ordinary footballers, for when he pushed from behind, always of course with an iron hook, it meant weeping and wailing, and gnashing of teeth to his unfortunate victim.

'No matter how his victim took it, Bruce always perceived a calm, unruffled countenance.'

There's no doubt that a tight marking contest with a hook-wielding opponent would result in 'weeping and wailing', but did he really take a hook onto the field? Aside from the Marshall quote there is not a single contemporary mention of Bruce and his hook. It's unlikely that Marshall made up the fact that Bruce had one arm and liked to whack opponents with a hook, but perhaps he conflated things: perhaps Bruce wore the hook in his day-to-day activities but took it off during the game. Newspaper articles that include Alex Bruce don't mention his hook, although that would really be something a reporter would jot down into their notebook.

Bruce seems to have been around for the founding of the sport. In May 1859 the Melbourne Cricket Club wrote down the first rules of the game – there were 10 rules, and none of them explained what sort of ball was to be used – and Bruce's signature is included on the first page. It looks as though he played for Melbourne and moved over to Fitzroy in 1860, and he pops up in a few match reports.

In late May 1859 *The Argus* reported on 'an excellent game of football' at the Melbourne Cricket Ground, a game for which Bruce had to rope in people hanging around the place to make up the numbers and he kicked the only goal in the match. In June that year there was a report of the Melbourne club's weekly game on the Richmond Paddock: 'Sides were selected by Mr Hammersley and Mr Bruce, and after some three hours' kicking three goals were obtained – two by Mr Hammersley's side and one by that of Mr Bruce,' *Bell's Life* reported. If only one of those mentions had included a photo of the guy, which would clear up the whole hook thing.

Incidentally, there has been a one-armed footy player, although without a hook. In 1954, 17-year-old Royce Dickson found himself picked up by Geelong and there was talk that he'd make his way into the top side. That talk ended in March of that year when he got his arm caught in the rollers of a mechanical blower at the wool mill where he worked. The rollers tore off his arm 10 centimetres below his shoulder, ending his chances at the Cats. A fundraiser for Dickson was held, with Geelong donating £100 to the fund and players presenting the hospital-bound Dickson with an electric razor. In 1954 that would have been a new-fangled gizmo and a flash present for the times.

He might not have made the top grade at Geelong, but Dickson didn't give up on footy. In April 1956 he took the field for Golden Square against Sandhurst in the Bendigo League reserve grade competition. He impressed the judges, being voted best on ground in his team's 27-point win. Later that year he got the call-up to the firsts but was forced to leave the field with the game just a few minutes old after injuring himself in a collision with an opponent.

In 1956 Dickson had a big win when he took wool mill owner Collins Bros to the Geelong Supreme Court. By then a student teacher, Dickson was awarded £5,000 in compensation: the equivalent of $182,000 in today's money.

2

BOB MURPHY'S MEDAL

It's the moment most people remember from the 2016 grand final, the moment when Bulldogs coach Luke Beveridge called the injured heartbeat of the club, Bob Murphy, to the dais after the Dogs had beaten Sydney 13.11 (89) to 10.7 (67). It's a moment that will live on forever in people's memories and the history of the sport, but there was so much history to overcome for that moment to happen. For so long the Dogs had been the sort of team that was never quite good enough; their last flag had been in 1954, when they beat Melbourne by 51 points. Their last visit to the big dance had been in 1961, when they lost to Hawthorn; footy geeks will know that was the first grannie not to feature a VFL foundation club.

In living memory the Dogs had been a team that seemed far more likely of going out of the competition altogether rather than going all the way. In the mid-1980s the club had been full of debt, but it somehow managed to stay on its feet. Things hadn't improved by 1989, when the VFL and some on the board entertained the idea of a merger with Fitzroy as a lifeline. Despite dwindling attendance at home games that year that suggested the fans had turned their backs on the Dogs they launched a fightback helmed by later premiership president Peter Gordon. The courts granted an injunction to stop the merger and give supporters and the club a chance to pull themselves out of debt. Somehow, they did it: the Dogs' fighting spirit saw more than 10,000 attend a rally at the Western Oval, and within three weeks more than $1.6 million had been raised.

The 1990s brought a more competitive version of the Dogs, and more heartbreak too. Western Bulldogs sides made the preliminary final in 1992, 1997 and 1998 only to lose them all. The 1997 match perhaps hurt more than most: playing under the Western Bulldogs name for the first season, they lost to the Crows by the slender margin 12.21 (93) to 13.13 (91). They went into the match raging favourites to reach their first grand final since forever, but the Crows got it all together in the final quarter to kick four goals to none for a come from behind win. It cemented the Dogs' image, both to their fans and others, as the team that would never quite be good enough and saw an approach among fans that for whatever reason the Dogs just weren't going to be allowed to have nice things.

It wasn't pessimism, but was the reality of supporting the Dogs. In his book *A Wink from the Universe* Martin Flanagan quoted Bulldogs historian Ace Arthur's view that defeat was synonymous with the Doggies: 'We've had five decades of it. You don't want to accept defeat, but you have to.' Not only did the 2016 squad have to shake off the idea, burnished to a shine through the club's history, that defeat was always hiding in the shadows waiting to waylay the Dogs, they also had to overcome more recent events that should have crippled a team certain the fates forever had it in for them.

The sports media always like the sound of the phrase a 'club in crisis', and they attached that to the Dogs in the 2014 off season. The sportswriters were also no doubt happy the Dogs had given them something to write about when there was no footy being played. That season the Dogs finished in 14th place on the ladder, with just seven wins. Team captain Ryan Griffen left the Bulldogs in October, heading to the GWS Giants. His justification was that the captaincy had ruined his love of footy: 'I found myself in a hole,' he told afl.com.au after becoming a Giant. 'If I'd stayed at the Bulldogs for another 12 months I would have ended up leaving the game . . . I'm getting a bit emotional about it but I needed a change.'

At the same time coach Brendan McCartney resigned, amid rumours that the captain walking out didn't speak well for his role going forward. Despite losing the Dogs captain and coach in the same week, Peter Gordon insisted it wasn't time to jump into the lifeboats: it wasn't a crisis, just a tough week in the office he said, though he admitted post-premiership that, yeah, it *was* a crisis. Of course it was, but the Bulldogs made their way out of it by appointing a new coach in Luke Beveridge. A journeyman footballer, he'd played 31 games for the Bulldogs in a 118-game career across three different clubs. As a coach his success rate was much better: he had been involved in six premierships in eight seasons, including those when he was on the coaching staff at Collingwood and Hawthorn.

One of Beveridge's first jobs was finding a new captain, but rather than picking one himself he looked to get the players involved. 'We will make sure that the decision will be a collaborative one, and that means with the players and the coaching staff,' he said to the *Herald Sun*. The smart money was always on Bob Murphy, who had been with the club since making his debut in 2000, as guiding the team out of the turmoil of 2014 would take an older, wiser head. After he got the job Murphy admitted he felt it was his time. 'It had never been a burning ambition for me but with the last couple of months and Griff walking away, I felt compelled to step forward and I haven't doubted that instinct for a second since,' he said in the *Cairns Post*.

Those decisions made in the off season ended up bearing fruit in 2015. A season that was birthed in crisis saw the Dogs win twice as many matches as the previous season for a sixth-place finish. Although the history books showed they were knocked out in the first week of the finals, at the start of the season who really had expected them to even *be* in the finals?

Things looked on the up for the Dogs for the 2016 season, and that feeling lasted until the final minute of the third round against the Hawks. The Dogs were sitting at the top of the ladder courtesy of big wins in the first two rounds and looked to have the measure of the previous season's premiers, then the captain's knee went with just 70 seconds left in the game. Murphy had got tangled up with Hawk Luke Breust and reeled out of it immediately, holding his knee and hopping on one foot. The diagnosis that eventually came indicated a season-ending cruciate ligament injury, but Murphy knew how bad it was from the moment he got tangled up with Breust. 'I was as certain as you can be,' he said in a media conference the next day. 'I felt the pop. I'm just letting it all wash over me at the moment. It has been a pretty heartbreaking 24 hours.'

After that game many Dogs fans figured the fates had whacked them yet again, tricking them into entertaining foolish dreams of success only to pull the rug out from under them. All the pundits figured they could rule a line through the Dogs for 2016; it was Beveridge's task to ensure that didn't happen. He was the right man for the job, leavening toughness with a strong understanding of the emotional heft of what had happened. 'We did talk about it. I think the players were more emotional about Bob than the loss, and that's understandable,' the coach told *The Age*. 'There's an opportunity out there for someone, and for all of us, to spread that load. The message will be no different and then we'll probably challenge them a little bit to support each other.'

Rather than fall into a heap the Dogs rose, winning 13 of their remaining 19 matches to land in seventh spot at the end of the home and away season, but still the fates were against them: no team had won the flag from that spot on the ladder. While the Bulldogs players surely knew that, they played like no one had told them it wasn't possible. They travelled to Perth to take down the Eagles in an elimination final, then took care of business against Hawthorn a week later. That brought them into the dreaded preliminary final, the hurdle so many other Dogs teams had not been able to overcome.

The team had to travel again, this time to Sydney to play the Giants. In a tight match the Giants got 14 points in front in the final quarter, the biggest margin in the game, but the Dogs wouldn't go away and levelled the scores at 82 a piece with five minutes left. Jack Macrae kicked a goal for the Dogs, only his second for the season, and the team held off a desperate Giants side to win 13.11 (89) to 12.11 (83).

The Dogs were heading to their first grand final in more than 50 years, and while they told themselves not to Dogs fans started to dream. For one person the dream came with a streak of torture: Murphy was in a strange position, as he was part of the team but keenly aware he would be sitting in the stands watching his team-mates on the Melbourne Cricket Ground turf rather than being down there among them. 'I can't help feeling cheated out of my destiny,' he wrote in his autobiography, *Leather Soul*, of waking up on grand final morning, 'that I've dedicated a good chunk of my heart, body and soul to my football club and just as we're about to walk into the sunshine, I'm shackled in the shadows.'

He decided to wear his jersey underneath his club polo shirt, and as he pulled it over his head his wife Justine walked into the bedroom. No words were said – there was no need – and his wife left the room in tears.

It would be a hell of a game, with the score tight through to the final quarter when a Jason Johannisen goal from the 50 allowed the Dogs to open up a 13-point lead with six minutes on the clock. The faithful in the crowd roared, sure this had locked in the trophy, but the cruel fates chose to intervene. After a long amount of time the goal was disallowed on a score review, which cut the lead back to eight. 'The Dogs supporters are dismayed,' Dennis Cometti said in the commentary. 'They fear things like this.'

It seemed like yet another hurdle had been put in the way of glory, but the Dogs on the field didn't care: from the Swans kick out Jordan Roughead marked in the centre square in the middle of three Swans and sent it back downfield. Just on a minute later Dale Morris chased down Buddy Franklin and caused a turnover. Tom Boyd picked it up on the half-forward line and kicked to an open goal, and it bounced through. In that minute the Dogs players looked the fates square in the face – and gave them the finger.

From there it was all over, helped by a Swans miss from a set shot with four and a bit minutes on the clock. The scent of victory can be intoxicating, can provide a lift: the Bulldogs were running as hard at the end of the game as they had been after the first bounce. With just over two minutes to go Jake Stringer centred a kick to Liam Picken in the goal square, and Picken gathered the ball in and drilled it for six. 'It's over, it's all over,' Bruce McAvaney said. 'The drought . . . the dam wall has busted.' The cameras start scanning the ground, finding people in red, white and blue who were wiping the tears from their faces and hugging partners and parents who had waited so long for this.

More tears came at the medal presentation, in a moment that is remembered by many just as clearly as anything that happened during the match. After Beveridge accepted the Jock McHale Medal he ran through a list of thank yous: the Swans players, his players, the sponsors, the officials, the fans and the Dogs back room and front office staff. He then moved to walk off the dais, but something came to him in the moment that caused him to stop and return to the microphone. 'Before I go,' he said as he took off his medal, 'I'd like to get Bob Murphy up on the stand.' The crowd roared and Beveridge waited as Murphy's team-mates hugged him. 'This is yours, mate, you deserve it more than anyone.'

Murphy walked onto the stage and was greeted by stand-in captain Easton Wood. Their hug was not the general sort of sporting hug you usually see but one full of emotion, caring and respect. Beveridge draped his medal around Murphy's neck, a moment that resonated because it was about love. That word is never mentioned in the alpha male world of Australian Football League (AFL) footy, but that was what it was. Back when Murphy had been injured Beveridge had said, 'There's a lot of man love between Bob and I.' There was a lot of love in the Dogs camp in general. Wood expressed similar emotions about Murphy after the win: 'He's very close to me, I just love him,' he told *The Age* after the match.

To amplify the medal gesture the coach took a step back as the premiership trophy was presented to let Murphy take his place and lift it to the heavens. The injured captain praised his coach's generosity: after feeling like he had been hiding in the shadows during grand final week, Beveridge had brought Murphy out into the light.

At the same time people praised Beveridge's selfless act some in the media looked to cheapen it by suggesting the AFL should issue a second medal to the coach. Part of the special nature of the gesture was that there was only one medal and the coach chose to give it to someone he thought was deserving. Creating a second one would have made Beveridge's gesture meaningless.

As it was, Murphy returned the medal a week later. 'I put him in a difficult situation, but he had to have recognition,' Beveridge said at the Charles Sutton Medal presentation. 'He returned the Jock McHale Medal. He said he couldn't keep it but he thanked me for the gesture.' The coach decided it wasn't his medal either, and gave it to the club museum. Beverige got his own honour in short time, when the Sport Australia Hall of Fame presented him with the Spirit of Sport Award. It wasn't presented every year, but only when the Hall of Fame panel found a truly outstanding candidate.

The Dogs were not the only sporting team that broke a drought in 2016. In the National Rugby League competition the Cronulla Sharks won their first grand final since entering the competition in 1967, and in the UK Leicester City took out the Premier League title for the first time in its 132-year history. The Chicago Cubs broke a 108-year-old curse when they won the Major League Baseball crown, while in the National Basketball Association the Cleveland Cavaliers became champions after 46 years. Finally, after 21 years the Hurricanes took out the Super Rugby title. Throw in Portugal's first-ever tournament win at Euro 2016 and it truly was the year of the underdogs.

AFTER HISSING THE FILM, THE THEATREGOERS LAUGHED AT IT,' THE *DAILY TELEGRAPH* REPORTED.

3

A VERY CHITTY MOVIE

On the field only a fool would laugh at Bob Chitty, for Bob was a hard, hard man. He revelled in the punchfest that was the 1945 grand final, flooring at least two opponents before one of their team-mates evened the score by levelling the halfback flanker. He played the role of the very hard man throughout his 146-game career and clearly showed a canny knack for getting in his licks while the umpire was looking the other way: he spent just 16 weeks on the sidelines through suspension for offences such as elbowing and striking

The website australianfootball.com put it quite well: 'Bob Chitty was one of the toughest, most fearsomely aggressive footballers ever to take the field. Some players manufacture aggression, others seem born to it; as far as Bob Chitty was concerned aggression oozed out of his every pore.'

Laughing at him on the field was very bad, but laughing at him on the big screen? That was fine; in fact, it was warranted. For reasons understood by pretty much nobody – perhaps not even the man himself – Chitty decided to take on the role of Ned Kelly in a movie. 'No, I don't know why I was selected to have a shot at the part,' he told *Melbourne Herald* football writer Alf Brown. 'I just happened to be Johnny on the spot. Of course, I could always ride, as before I came down to Carlton in 1937 I lived in good horse country at Cudgewa [in rural Victoria, up against the New South Wales border]. In those days you had to have a horse to get anywhere.'

When Chitty signed on for the role in 1947 he had been a year gone from Carlton and coaching the Benalla Saints (now playing in the Goulburn Valley Football League). That was handy, because he would have needed a lot of time off: shooting for the movie started in 1947 and the punters didn't get to see it until 1951, because there was more drama going on behind the cameras than in front of them.

Chitty had agreed to play Ned Kelly in *A Message to Kelly*, directed by Harry Southwell. Born in Wales, Southwell spent part of his life working in America as a screenwriter but upon the move to Australia he began making up a new persona, branding himself as a renowned director nicknamed the 'Welsh wizard'. This was despite the inconvenient fact that he had not directed a damned thing. However, he made up for lost time in that area, latching onto the Ned Kelly story and squeezing everything he could out of it. In 1919 he shot *The Kelly Gang*; the film reviewer for the *Yass Courier*, who believed most of their job involved relaying the entire plot, found it 'a magnificent production, and held the audience spellbound'.

In 1922 Southwell went back to the Kelly well, making *When the Kellys Were Out*. '[S]tory rather vague. Lack of detail' stated the review in *Smith's Weekly*. Southwell told another variation on the story with 1934's *When the Kellys Rode*, the first talking Kelly movie. It was several years before some people saw it; the New South Wales police didn't much care for bushranger flicks, talking or otherwise, and banned it. 'Anything that glorifies crime and criminals or suggests bringing constituted authority into a wrong light is not desirable in the public interest,' the police minister, Frank Chaffey, said, sounding like someone who was probably no fun at parties.

The move was total hypocrisy, as K.O. Fowles from Southwell's production company pointed out: 'Every day the public sees American films glorifying the gangster and the outlaw but apparently no exception is taken to these.' The police, though, might have done Southwell a favour: when the movie was finally released in the 1940s it got panned as a 'woefully comic curiosity' by the *Daily Telegraph* critic.

When it came to 1947 Southwell was out scouting locations for *A Message to Kelly*. In Benalla he bumped into Rupert Kathner, who was looking to shoot his own Kelly movie (jeez, the Australian film industry at the time wasn't keen on fresh ideas). To kill off a competing film Southwell got Kathner to work on his film instead, and Chitty started work filming a bank hold-up in the town of Tatong [in the foothills of the Great Dividing Range in Victoria]. 'Canvas chairs were set up in the main street and a few minutes later make-up men were busy with spirit gum and crepe hair transforming the clean shaven features of Bob Chitty into the bearded Ned Kelly,' the *Corryong Courier* reported.

That unnamed reporter was clearly overwhelmed by being in the proximity of a real-life movie shoot. 'One could almost believe that it was the genuine thing, as these four determined-looking men rode towards the bank,' they wrote. 'A curt command from the leader and the horses came to a halt, then a moment later Ned had smashed into the small building, to appear a moment later carrying the loot.'

Southwell and Kathner had a falling out when the former realised the latter was still going to make his own Kelly movie, so he sacked the director. A few weeks later Southwell had run out of money and his *A Message to Kelly* film came to an end. In 1950 Kathner was back in Benalla to shoot his effort, *The Glenrowan Affair*. Chitty was still keen to come on board as Ned: after all, the break had given him time to grow a nice, big bushranger beard.

The story is told in flashback from the point of view of Ned's brother Dan Kelly, sitting in Benalla. While Dan actually died in Glenrowan there are some conspiracy theorists who believe he may have escaped but, rest assured, there were other elements of dodginess going on in *The Glenrowan Affair*. A title card announced the Glenrowan siege at Ann Jones' hotel as taking place in 1887, which would be a neat trick given Kelly was hanged seven years earlier. In another scene there is a Victoria Bitter sign on a wall, but the brand didn't exist until the 1890s. There were also numerous other instances where Kathner rejigged historical events or just made things up.

In April 1952 the film got a special screening in Benalla's open-air theatre. Police patrolled the theatre, having heard rumours that Kelly's descendants planned to break up the screening. They didn't show up, but the crowd's response could hardly have been worse if they had: they ridiculed the film, and Chitty's acting. 'After hissing the film, the theatregoers laughed at it,' the *Daily Telegraph* reported. The *Adelaide News* reported a similar story, through quotes from local copper Senior Constable G. Haag: 'In one of the early scenes of the film one of the characters appeared wearing a zip-fronted jacket and he was opening a tin of sardines, no less,' Haag said. 'These modern items in a historical picture sent the audience into gales of laughter.'

The reviewer in the Sydney *Sun-Herald* gave *The Glenrowan Affair* a pasting: 'This near-unendurable stretch of laboured, amateurish film-making is something that the developing Australian film industry will wish to forget swiftly and finally. The script is dreary, the photography more often out-of-focus than in, the editing is unimaginative and the acting petrified. It would be misplaced kindness, in fact, to try and ferret out a redeeming feature.'

For those hardy souls keen to check out Chitty's work there are short segments of the movie available on YouTube, which is probably the best you can do unless you want to pay a high price for a DVD copy on eBay – but why pay that much money for a film you *already know* is going to be awful?

WHAT THE CLUB HAD BASED THEIR BRIBERY CLAIMS ON WAS A STING OPERATION INVOLVING A TEAM-MATE OF LANG'S.

4

GAMBLING WITH YOUR CAREER

By 1910 Alexander Lang had experienced a pretty good footy career for one so young. He debuted for Carlton in 1906 as an 18-year-old rover and was part of the Blues' flag that year, then Carlton pulled off a threepeat, winning in 1907 and 1908. Carlton and Lang missed the chance for a fourth straight title by just two points to South Melbourne in the 1909 decider, 4.14 (38) to 4.12 (36). Lots of shots went wide in that game, although sections of the media thought so highly of Lang that they named him the best player in the competition.

As he was walking into the Melbourne Cricket Ground sheds on 17 September 1910 to get ready for the semi-final against South Melbourne, Lang must have been on top of the world: at just 22 years of age he'd already won three premierships and was looking likely to add to that again. As was his practice Lang headed towards the wall where the team list was pinned, thinking as he did so how odd it was that all his team-mates were looking at him without saying a word. When he read over the list he didn't see his name in at rover, or at the ruck; it wasn't there at all. He asked the club officials what was going on and they told him straight: they knew he'd been bribed and the club wasn't going to let him play. He wasn't alone, as childhood friend and team-mate Doug Gillespie was also stood down, as was Doug Fraser.

Carlton had been a bit tricky with that semi-final team list. They had known at mid-week that something funny was going on, yet in order not to tip off those who had organised the fix the club named Lang, Gillespie and Fraser – even releasing the list earlier than usual so the papers could run it. Without their star rover Carlton lost to a much more accurate South Melbourne 10.5 (65) to 6.17 (53). That prompted one Carlton supporter to point out that by omitting those players the club created the very thing the crims were hoping for: a South Melbourne win. Worse still was to come: that Saturday afternoon Lang's charmed life as a football player was effectively over, all for accepting a few pounds.

The day after the semi-final Lang chose to go on the offensive and have a nice long chat with *The Argus* newspaper journalist who had lobbed up on his dad's front verandah: 'I was approached in the street by a man who asked me 'will you run a bye' [throw the game],' Lang said. 'I refused and then I thought as he was trying to play a game on me I would turn the tables. He wanted me to run the bye as he called it and to pay up afterwards, but I demanded the money. After some argument, he handed me £10. I had not the money in my possession 10 minutes. I gave it to a friend to back Carlton.'

Lang also said he could never run on the field without trying and hadn't wanted to tell the club about the bribe, because if he played below his normal standards it would think he had made up the bribe as an excuse. Lang also cleared Gillespie, saying he 'is as innocent as a babe in the matter', while Fraser was approached but took no money.

As it turned out Lang's attempt to get out in front of this looming scandal was a mistake. The club hadn't known anything about the bribe from a man in the street, so in talking about it Lang dumped himself in the poo big time. What the club had based their bribery claims on was a sting operation involving a team-mate of Lang's. On the Monday before the semi-final forward Jack Baquie (or Bacquie) told the club he'd received a letter from a shopkeeper offering cash if he would 'run a bye'. While the paper gently referred to the letter writer as 'a certain city shopkeeper', they meant he was a bookie and the shop he kept was a betting shop. On Thursday Baquie and the bookie were due to meet again, so the club sent someone to spy on the shop. This Carlton spy claimed that when Baquie left the shop he bumped into Lang and Fraser as they were entering.

That seems to have been the sum total of evidence the club had of bribery: players walking into a betting shop. Fraser always denied accepting any cash, while Lang appeared to have thought the club was talking about something else and stitched himself up. The club conducted its own inquiry in the days after the semi, deciding Gillespie was in the clear. As for Lang and Fraser, Carlton officials made the useless ruling that those two couldn't play until further notice. It was a decision that answered nothing: if they were innocent of bribery why suspend them, and if they were guilty of it why *only* suspend them?

Clearly the Victorian Football League (VFL) was going to have to get involved, which seemed blindingly obvious from the outset. That happened, and the initial plan was to allow the press in to report the proceedings. That was quickly bashed on the head when a witness spoke of allegations that Henry Skinner, the very well-off president of South Melbourne, had offered his team cash if they won. Of course, that was a scurrilous allegation, as no official would pay their players. Yes, that's sarcasm: they were *all* paying their players.

To shut down any risk of the papers reporting on Skinner's slippery dealings, he told the league the inquiry had to go behind closed doors – not because of him, but rather because the witnesses might be less open if they knew their words were going to appear in newspaper coverage. In the end Skinner got his way, and it's not known what evidence the league had to make them take the course of action they did. It was a very rough course of action, handed down at 11.30 pm the night before the VFL grand final: Lang and Fraser were disqualified for five years, until 31 December 1915.

The ban meant the pair wouldn't be on the field for the grand final, lost to Collingwood 9.7 (61) to 6.11 (47). They would miss what one paper called 'another of those disgraceful exhibitions for which the season has become noted'. Things got hairy going into the final term: with Collingwood ahead by 20 points, Carlton figured a little of the rough stuff might unsettle them. When Baquie and Collingwood's Tom Baxter contested a mark, the Carlton forward cocked a fist and let fly when the pair hit the ground. Jack Shorten and Les Hughes from Collingwood and Carlton's Percy Sheehan arrived on the scene and got stuck into it as well.

'A stand-up fight was in progress in the centre of the field,' the *Kalgoorlie Miner* reported. 'The remainder of the players were running to the scene, and then the [ground] attendants joined in the chase. The police bolted from the sides and 20 or 30 men from the rival camps jumped over the fence and set out to join in the fight.' It was only the clever actions of umpire Jack Elder that defused things by blowing his whistle fiercely, taking the ball out to the wing and bouncing it up. Baquie, Sheehan, Baxter and Shorten all met up again at the VFL investigations committee a few days later. Baxter and Baquie were banned for the 1911 season, while the other two received 18-month bans.

These were severe punishments, but those players' suspensions ended well before Lang's. For Lang and any other player the temptation to take whatever cash was offered would have been exacerbated by the fact that in the early years of the VFL players were expected to be amateurs. They were to play for the love of the sport rather than expect some sort of compensation, despite the fact there were risks that an injury on the field might see them not be able to carry out their day job. The clubs, though, were allowed to make money out of the game from the efforts of the players, who actually brought people through the gate.

It had been that way for a decade, ever since the three-year-old VFL decided paying players was a big no-no. At a May 1900 meeting representatives of the clubs passed a motion that stated 'Any player receiving payment, directly or indirectly, for his services as a footballer, shall be disqualified for any period the league may decide, and any club paying a player, either directly or indirectly, for his services as a footballer, shall be dealt with as the league may think fit.' Pretty much every club was slinging players cash under the table, so they wouldn't go hard on another club that got caught lest their own dealings were revealed.

Lang, a triple premiership player, was never allowed to legally profit from his skills, so it's no wonder he opted to take that £10. What probably stung Lang more was that in the wake of his and Fraser's ousting the league began debating whether Rule 29, the one that forbade paying players, should be scrapped. A vote before the start of the 1911 season saw it kept in place, then just ahead of round three the vote went the other way and the floodgates were open for player payments while Lang was sitting on the sidelines. He did try to get back into the game, lodging appeals against the five-year ban, but after being refused for four years in a row he read the writing on the wall and served out the remainder of his sentence.

Lang finally returned in 1916 to play for the club that had banned him, but it was a very different team from the one he had last played for in 1910: there were just three team-mates he knew from those days. It was a changed competition as well. Because of World War I Essendon, Geelong, South Melbourne, Melbourne and St Kilda all declined to play, which left a competition made up of just four teams: Carlton, Fitzroy, Collingwood and Richmond. With teams playing each other four times it resulted in the bizarre situation where the 1916 wooden spooners were also the premiers. Fitzroy ended the regular season in last place with two wins, a draw and nine losses but clicked into gear in the post season, winning three straight matches to claim the flag.

Lang wasn't the same player either; at the age of 28 he was lacking in match fitness. That was something a few in the media never let him forget, regularly writing jibes about how the former champion was carrying too much weight. In his first match, the opening-round clash against Fitzroy, the *Football Record* was especially cruel: '[Lang] hit the ground hard as a result of a hearty bump. His fat right arm was grazed by the ground and looked as if it had been pecked by a fowl. Lang requires a lot of hard training to take off much of his weight, as he now tips the beam at 13 stone, 4 pounds [84 kg].'

That hardly seems overweight, which makes a comment from another *Football Record* writer that he needed to lose around 50 kilograms, leaving him a playing weight of just 34 kilograms, nonsensical. That same writer, the pseudonymous 'Wideawake', also saw fit to ridicule Lang's size by saying he had to wear captain Billy Dick's No. 1 jersey, because his own didn't fit. 'After 17 [players] had gone out, a fat man came on in a guernsey bearing Billy Dick's number, the rotund one was Alex Lang.'

The reality was that while his years away from the game had inevitably taken its toll, Lang still had enough football knowledge between his ears to make his way around the field. He also adapted to his new position in the forward pocket as well as kicking goals, his football brain allowing him to set up team-mates for a six pointer. His last game was on 9 June 1917, against Fitzroy, and he left the VFL with 105 matches under his belt.

Things were much worse for his banished team-mate Fraser, who never played in the VFL again. Just months after the ban he was charged with using obscene language outside the Railway Hotel in Yarraville after being ejected. According to the court he was 'making use of the most filthy and obscene expressions' with dozens of people nearby, 'including women and children, who could hear what was said'. Fraser scarpered to New South Wales but was picked up on a warrant when he returned to Victoria. The court found him guilty and fined him £10. He later fell victim to the 1918 influenza epidemic that had gripped the country, dying on 24 February 1919 at the age of 32.

WANT TO DISCOVER THE WORST TEAM IN AUSTRALIAN FOOTY HISTORY? COMING UP!

GEELONG ESPECIALLY SEEMED TO LOVE TAKING THE EARLY ST KILDA SIDES TO THE CLEANERS.

5

THE WORST TEAM EVER

When it comes to deciding on the worst footy team in history the St Kilda side of 1897–1902 is a definite contender. In fact, they may win the award, as it's hard to imagine another side surpassing their ineptitude. In those six seasons, their first in the AFL, St Kilda managed to win just two games and lost an incredible 97. Their first three seasons in the league were winless, so they started their existence with a 48-match losing streak. There were certainly some embarrassing defeats in those early years. In St Kilda's third-ever game, South Melbourne rolled them 8.11 (59) to 0.2 (2). Later that season Essendon humiliated them 13.16 (94) to 0.3 (3).

Geelong especially seemed to love taking the early St Kilda sides to the cleaners. In round seven of the 1897 season Geelong thumped them 16.18 (114) to 4.7 (31) and decided to whack them again later that season 14.12 (96) to 3.0 (18). The second season was no better: St Kilda got thumped 13.15 (93) to 3.7 (25) and 14.18 (102) to 4.3 (27). In the 1899 season Geelong totally went to town on the hapless St Kilda – twice. The first meeting ended with a 16.23 (119) to 0.2 (2) final score. According to one match report St Kilda was so bad hardly anyone turned up to watch. 'Not very much interest was manifested in the match between Geelong and St Kilda played at Geelong,' reported the Melbourne *Herald*, 'the attendance at the oval being rather small.'

The journalist didn't stop there: 'Since the establishment of the league they [St Kilda] have failed to score a single win, and Geelong and the other leading clubs have very little cause to fear them. The fact that they have remained together despite their long run of failure speaks well for them as sportsmanlike footballers and none would regret a turn in the tide for them.'

That tide wasn't going to change any time soon. If St Kilda's woeful two behinds in that match against Geelong wasn't bad enough, they were even worse in the second clash. St Kilda travelled to Geelong's Corio Oval, though it's hard to understand why they bothered. The visitors took an early lead courtesy of a behind. And then didn't score another point – seriously, their final score was 0.1 (1). As for Geelong, they were busy racking up a massive 162 points, via 23 goals and 24 behinds; if their forwards' boots were more accurate, the scoreline would have *really* blown out.

The Argus summed it all up with their headline 'A Slaughter of Innocents'. *The Age* tried valiantly to find a bright side to the debacle: 'So well did the Saints acquit themselves in the first quarter of an hour that they actually scored the first point, but this proved their initial and also concluding success, for after that period Geelong simply took the play into their own hands and the Saints went onto their fate as an ox goeth to the slaughter.'

Any followers St Kilda had were forced to wait until round one of the 1900 season for their team to win, and even then – due a bizarre turn of events – they didn't get to enjoy it immediately after the final siren sounded. Played in a strong wind at the Junction Oval, the scoring went with the breeze. St Kilda put up a 36-point lead on Melbourne at the end of the first quarter; the visitors had only kicked two behinds into the wind. In the second quarter Melbourne made the most of the wind, creeping ahead by six points after keeping the home side scoreless.

The match evened out after half-time when the wind died down. When the umpire called time the home side had kicked 10.8 (68) to the visitors' 9.14 (68), a draw, but the St Kilda officials lodged a protest, claiming a behind was incorrectly awarded to Melbourne. At a meeting of the league's investigation committee at the Port Phillip Hotel later that night the protest was upheld and St Kilda was awarded the one-point win, its first in the VFL, though most of their fans went to bed after the game thinking their team had drawn with Melbourne.

Incidentally, St Kilda has been on the wrong end of another infamous score, in the round 12, 1919 match against South Melbourne. The Saints got annihilated 29.15 (189) to 2.6 (18), and the way it happened raised eyebrows. In the final quarter South Melbourne kicked an astonishing 15 goals to put on 106 points while keeping St Kilda scoreless. 'Though far from being a good game, the match between South Melbourne and St Kilda on the South Melbourne cricket ground proved to be one of the most remarkable of the season,' *The Argus* reported. 'Its main feature of interest was the rapidity and certainty with which South Melbourne scored towards the end of the match when St Kilda's resistance had practically broken down.'

... WHAT HAPPENS ON THE FIELD STAYS ON THE FIELD ... YOU CAN CLOCK SOMEONE ON THE PLAYING FIELD AND THE RULE OF LAW DOESN'T APPLY.

6

IT'S A KNOCKOUT

When a player runs on the field at the start of a game it's unlikely they're thinking that they might do something out there that would result in jail time. That's in no small part due to the belief that what happens on the field stays on the field, that you can clock someone on the playing field and the rule of law doesn't apply. Of course, that goes both ways: there is also no rule of law for the team-mates of the clocked player, so they can make their aggressor's on-field afternoon quite painful.

On 20 March 1911 that rule didn't seem to apply to Carlton rover Martin Gotz. What he allegedly did against a University player in the last quarter was serious enough to see him staring in the face of a jail sentence: he levelled Vic Trood, knocking him unconscious. 'League football was again disgraced on Saturday by one of those incidents [that] degraded the game last season,' *The Argus* stated in the first line of its story. 'In the final quarter of the match between University and Carlton, Trood, a University player, was felled to the earth in front of the reserve at the Melbourne Cricket Ground by a cowardly and unprovoked assault. He was stunned and carried off the field, and for some time lay in the dressing-room unconscious.'

As is expected when something shocking happened on the field, the story ran in papers across the country and they all commenced hand-wringing about how awful it was that such a thing happened while knowing it was exactly the sort of thing that would grab its readers. An interstate paper, *The Examiner*, ran a more detailed description of what had transpired and that it caused 'a howl of indignation all round the ground': 'In a crush in which [Jack] Wells and Gotz, of Carlton, and Trood, of University, were striving Trood had just kicked the ball, when Gotz closed in on him from one side and Wells from the other. An arm shot up to his jaw with a deliberate uppercut, and Trood fell as if he were dead, and was carried off the ground. So severe was the blow that after the finish of the match he was still dazed. It was one of the worst things ever seen on the football field.'

University was very unhappy with what had happened and immediately demanded Carlton take action. 'At a meeting of my committee, held after the match between the University and Carlton teams on Saturday last,' Seitz wrote in a letter to Carlton officials the day after the match, 'I was instructed to inform you that, in consequence of the behaviour of certain of your players my committee has decided to decline to play the return match with your team on the Carlton ground on Saturday, July 15, unless such players are excluded from your team.'

Five days after the match things got serious: a court summons was issued alleging Gotz had assaulted Trood. As far as University was concerned, this was definitely not going to be left on the field and the court case started in early July, with Trood not being able to help very much; he had no idea who had hit him.

Stockbroker and spectator Henry Alexander Dodd appeared for the prosecution, saying he saw Gotz give Trood 'a short-arm jolt under the chin' and that there was no confusion as to whose fist it had been: Gotz was wearing a long-sleeved jersey while his nearby Carlton team-mates, including Wells, were all sleeveless. The issue of the sleeves was a crucial factor for the prosecution, with several prosecution witnesses mentioning it. Dodd insisted that Gotz then ran back to his position after levelling Trood. All-up there were four witnesses at the game who insisted Gotz was the guilty party.

Gotz's defence lawyer's approach was to cloud the issue, stating it was quite possible Trood was hit by an accidental blow. Gotz took the stand and said he saw the ball on the wing, with two University players and one from Carlton fighting for it. Gotz said that as he ran to the pack at top speed he was fortunate to have the ball roll towards him. He picked it up, ran through the pack – claiming to have been kicked on the shin on the way – and kept going, which was when he met another University player who took him out of bounds. 'I did not put a finger on Trood,' Gotz said. 'It was not possible for me to touch him as I was running at my top [speed].'

A police officer named Absalom testified that he was around 30 metres from the spot where Trood had fallen and was sure Gotz had had nothing to do with it. He said no one was near Trood when he fell: 'There was no blow struck. Trood fell as the result of a collision.' Another officer, Constable Murray, said Gotz had run through the pack and was taken out of bounds, Trood hitting the deck around five seconds after Gotz had left.

When asked for his opinion Constable Murray stated he felt the collision with Wells was what had knocked out Trood. A third officer, Constable Calwell, said Gotz was shaping up to shoulder Trood but Wells beat him to it.

The issue of sleeves versus sleeveless guernseys came up via the evidence of merchant William Harper: 'Trood had been beating Wells. There was a scrimmage and I saw a bare arm come out. Wells hit Trood. It was not an uppercut, but a straight blow. Gotz was not within striking distance at the time. I thought the blow was an unsportsmanlike, rotten thing.' Evidently what had happened was as clear as mud: Trood had been hit by a man in a long-sleeved guernsey or a sleeveless version, or not hit at all, or copped a shoulder. It makes you appreciate today's video replays, otherwise all tribunal hearings would be as confusing as this.

The judge had the unenviable task of finding some sort of truth in all the testimony. He chose not to believe the evidence of three coppers and found Gotz guilty of 'a serious and unprovoked assault' and Gotz was hit with a £10 fine, around $1,400 in today's money. If he was unable to pay the fine he was staring down the barrel of two months in jail – unless he managed to get the decision reversed on appeal.

In the intervening period the VFL had debated whether they should hold their own investigation. Fortunately for Gotz, sanity prevailed and the league felt it might prejudice the court appeal. That appeal took almost three months to make it in front of a judge, after which time the fog around the incident hadn't lifted for Trood. 'About 10 minutes after the last quarter had begun I was playing halfback on the left wing,' he said.

'I saw the ball coming to me and I dashed for it and got it. I prepared to dash off with it when I felt a blow on the right jaw. I am not sure whether at the moment I still had the ball or had got rid of it. I could not see where the blow came from.'

The next thing Trood *could* remember was lying on a table in the sheds with four people looking down on him. His lack of any recall set the stage for another round of evidence where the prosecution witnesses insisted it was the long-sleeved arm of Gotz that had hit Trood, while the defence swore it was Wells, someone else or no one at all. This time around Wells also gave evidence, perhaps to try to clear his name. However, he muddied the waters further, claiming Trood had kicked the ball after their collision and that after Wells had followed the ball he turned and saw Trood lying prone on the ground. Of course, Gotz was nowhere in the vicinity.

Out of all of that confusion appeal judge Gurner managed to come to a decision. He noted that as in the original court case almost every witness told a different story, so for him there were three options: either Gotz whacked Trood, Wells whacked Trood or Wells accidentally knocked Trood over. However, he didn't need to figure out which version was correct, just whether or not Gotz did it.

'I am aware that people in the moment of a football match do lose their temper, and use violence or are reputed to do so,' he said, 'but I have heard nothing here to lead me to suppose there was any animosity between Trood and the others. I feel something almost approaching conviction that Gotz did not hit the man, but it is not necessary for me to go that far. I am not convinced that anybody actually struck Trood. At any rate, I am not convinced beyond reasonable doubt that Gotz struck Trood and for that reason it is my duty to allow the appeal and quash the conviction.'

Gotz managed to escape jail time with the help of Carlton, whom he tried to throw under a bus the following year when the club denied him a release to join St Kilda. Gotz had decided to leave after Carlton cut his pay from £3 to £2/10 shillings, a drop of less than $100. He somehow decided that the pay cut meant he was sacked and so stopped turning up for training, which obviously meant he wasn't picked to play.

At a league hearing in which Gotz appealed the Carlton refusal to let him go he said he had been paid £3 by the Blues for the last seven years. Keep in mind that the rule that allowed players to be paid had only come in the previous year, and that Gotz had just said Carlton had been paying players in contravention of league rules for at least five years. That should have been a bombshell: no player had openly claimed to have been paid illegally, but nothing happened. No one cared, not even Carlton's representative at the hearing, E. Page Kennedy, who didn't make the slightest effort to claim Gotz was lying. Instead, he was annoyed that the ungrateful Gotz forgot the club had spent £150 defending him in court the previous year. The absolute silence was the best indication the league knew players had always been paid, and they chose not to open that Pandora's box.

The league refused to grant Gotz a release, so in protest he sat out the rest of the season rather than play for Carlton. After his self-imposed year-long dummy spit Gotz returned to the Blues for the 1914 season, though not before he fully recuperated from a most unfortunate injury. When not looking to pocket some cash for playing footy Gotz held down a job at the Robur Tea warehouse in Clarendon Street, South Melbourne. At around 11.00 am on Christmas Eve the 27 year old caught the lift down from the 11th floor and stepped out on the ground floor for a short while before heading back into the lift. Before he was fully on board the lift started to ascend, crushing him against the wall. 'A fellow employee heard Gotz's shout and brought the lift to a standstill in time to avert a most serious accident,' *The Herald* reported.

Gotz copped the brunt of the uncooperative lift across the middle of his body and was taken to the Royal Melbourne Hospital. Doctors found he'd had a lucky escape, suffering little more than a few abrasions and internal bruising. After an hour at the hospital Gotz took a taxi home and presumably had a very quiet and still Christmas Eve.

PUTTING IN THE BOOT HAS LONG BEEN A TRADITION WHEN IT COMES TO THE COVERAGE OF AUSTRALIAN RULES.

7

ROUND 4 A SNORE

Reporters and pundits throwing stones at footy players may seem like a new thing, something that has been brought about by social media and people deciding that, yes, the world does in fact need to hear every thought that goes pinging about their heads, but you'd be wrong. Putting in the boot has long been a tradition when it comes to the coverage of Australian rules. As a case in point, look at page five of *The Argus* of 30 May 1910: with barely any ads, the page is nine columns of tiny print, as though the aim was to cram as many words as possible on a page.

On that page are match reports from round 4, and if *The Argus* coverage is to be believed those matches were not very good at all. 'An unsatisfactory day' one headline reads. 'Several games spoiled' says another. It gets worse: 'Another uninteresting game', 'Bad in every feature' and 'Unpleasant game at Carlton'. It seems pretty safe to say that round 4 sucked. A lot.

'The matches on Saturday were not particularly interesting,' wrote 'Observer' (footy writers at the time took up aliases, presumably to stop irate players from tracking them down). 'Several of the more important games were spoiled and in one or two instances, merit in the general play was not rewarded as it should have been.' In a move that will not surprise anyone with a familiarity of footy coverage, Observer felt most of the problem was down to 'weak umpiring': 'I do not for a moment suggest that the umpires deliberately neglect their duty,' he backtracked, 'though it has been very evident for years past that they do hesitate about reporting players for misconduct.'

Of course, after identifying the problem the next step for a footy pundit is to provide a solution, which is the whole point of bringing up the problem in the first place. The solution to this problem was that ex-players should pick up the whistle. 'One could name many men not long retired from the field who would make admirable umpires. They have not only what may be called the technical qualifications but the strength of mind, the strength of character and high intelligence, which are more valuable than a mere knowledge of the rules.

'The trouble is that many of those old players occupy social positions, are engaged in their professions and do not care to become professional umpires. Further public clamour and want of thought has made the duty a very unpleasant one. No man cares to submit himself to the mercies of a howling mob carried beyond all reason by local bias.'

Let's move onto that 'Unpleasant game at Carlton'. The first line doesn't mince words as to how lacklustre the affair was: 'It is long since I have seen a game that had less to recommend it, either as a public spectacle or an exhibition of athletic skill, than the match played on Princes Oval between Carlton and South Melbourne.' Most of the punters were disgusted with the 'dragging, tumbling, tussling exhibition' that had South up

0.5 (5) to 0.2 (2) at the first change. Yeah, nothing but behinds kicked in the first term: sure sounds unpleasant.

The second term was 'Bad in every feature', with South up 1.6 (12) to 1.5 (11). Carlton won the match, but everyone in the stands lost. As for 'Another uninteresting game', that was Collingwood versus Essendon, a match Prime Minister Andrew Fisher had the misfortune of attending. 'Described in the term commonly used around the ground at the finish, it was a "rotten game", yet so fast and hard that both sides had all the exercise they wanted by the time it was half over.' Essendon won by two points, thanks in large part to Collingwood's crappy kicking: their four goals were overshadowed by a whopping 17 behinds.

Only the Melbourne and St Kilda clash warranted any positivity from *The Argus* subeditors: 'A keen finish' the headline read, only to be tempered by a subhead noting 'The umpire assaulted'. Which story do you think most people actually cared about? Of course, it's what happened to umpire George Hastings (for more about this see Chapter 23).

In the last minutes of a close game St Kilda's George Morrissey took a mark but was encroached by Melbourne's Vin Coutie. Morrissey got his kick away and it went through the big sticks, but rather than playing something like advantage Hastings called it back and made Morrissey kick again. He missed the second time, and Melbourne won by three points.

'This incident caused the St Kilda followers to see all sorts of faults in Hastings' umpiring,' *The Argus* reported. 'He was certainly not a huge success, but it was not bad enough to have justified the attack made upon him on his return to the pavilion.

Someone in the crowd struck at him and Hastings promptly hit back. For half a minute or so there was a lively tussle, but the disturbance went no further . . . Whether the umpire is right or wrong, it is always a matter for regret that any blackguard who chooses to hit him is not brought before the police courts and made to pay the usual penalty.'

8

THE FANS OF FITZROY

In the 2006 qualifying final against the West Coast Eagles, Sydney's Michael O'Loughlin snapped a six-pointer after gathering a bouncing ball in the goal square. It wasn't anything special in and of itself, though it did send the Swans home with a squeaker of a win: 13.7 (85) to 12.12 (84). It was what happened immediately afterwards that everyone remembers. The hardcore Eagles fans were right behind those posts giving a serve to anyone in a red and white jersey, so when O'Loughlin booted the goal he ran straight at one of them and celebrated in his face.

That fan was Daniel Williams, who seemed shocked that a player had broken the fourth wall of sports and actually chosen to give a spray back at the spectators. 'I sort of backed away because I was not sure what was going to happen,' said the man who seemed not to be able to take what he dished out. 'At first I did feel threatened. You sort of hear where players have tried to take a swing or spit at people. I didn't know what was going to happen but all those things were in the back of my mind.'

When standing behind the posts Williams said he always kept an eye on the ball to make sure it didn't hit him, so he had his neck craned to follow its flight only to turn back to the field and find O'Loughlin staring right at him. 'Everyone is saying I shit myself but I was just surprised because you don't expect it to happen.'

To be fair to Williams, he was gracious when the *Daily Telegraph* called him in 2009 to say O'Loughlin had retired. 'Really, when did that happen?' Williams asked. 'That's sad. It's sad when any really great player hangs up his boots. I still get asked if I'm that guy in the photo with Micky O.' He also turned up on the TV show *The Front Bar* to recreate the iconic moment with O'Loughlin.

Once upon a time a barracker ran the risk of something far worse than a footy player getting in their face, with an incident from a 1902 Collingwood–Fitzroy clash making that very clear. It was round 11 at the Lions' Brunswick Street base and the home crowd was giving it to Collingwood rover Charlie Pannam. Why? Who knows: it's not like fans need a reason to berate the other side. Reports differ as to when Pannam did what he did; one said it was at half-time while another said it was during the game.

All reports agree on *what* he did: climb into the stands and whack someone. 'In the abstract of course, Pannam was guilty of misconduct,' *The Leader* said, 'but it must be remembered that a hiding is but mild punishment for the abusive and filthy language used by some of those disgusting people whose sole object in attending football matches seems to be to create a disturbance and who cannot be fair to the side for which they are not barracking.' *The Argus* added that the man's fellow

Fitzroy supporters urged him to report Pannam to the police but the victim declined, perhaps because on some level he figured he'd gotten what was coming to him.

If the news reports of Fitzroy home games are anything to go by, the Lions supporters in the early days were a nasty breed. In May 1908 when South played Fitzroy, someone in the crowd at the railway end of the Brunswick Street ground chucked a stone that managed to hit the central umpire in the head. While the news reports don't name which side the stone chucker supported, given that we'll soon see the Fitzroy supporter base at the time had form let's blame them for it.

In June that same year the Lions lost a tight one to Essendon 5.12 (42) to 5.8 (38). The home fans were incensed and jumped the fence to attack the visiting Essendon side. 'At one time the rush looked particularly venomous,' *The Herald* reported, 'and several of the Essendon men were bleeding when they reached their dressing room.'

A plainclothes police officer was trying to hold back the horde but Fitzroy player Bill Walker thought he was one of the thugs and was about to hit a team-mate, so Walker smashed the police officer in the face. The riot only calmed down after a Fitzroy fan stuck a pin in the rear of a police horse, which galloped around the ground with an officer holding on for dear life. The brawling stopped so everyone could watch that. However, a total sense of peace and goodwill hadn't fallen over Brunswick Street. A large crowd milled outside waiting for Essendon to leave, which they finally did after enough policemen arrived to escort them to waiting taxis and then on to safety.

Something similar happened in June 1909 against Melbourne. In a match won by the visitors and in which both teams threw punches at the other, the crowd looked to want in on the violence. 'At the finish there was an unpleasant and threatening scene,' *The Argus* wrote, 'for the crowd was angry and the police had to guard the Melbourne men to their dressing rooms, with a hustling crowd all about them and some young imps, who catch the infection from their seniors, arming themselves with stones.'

What they did with those stones is not known, but given the earlier stone chucking that hit an umpire in the scone we can imagine they were destined for someone's head.

9

A MISTAKEN MERGER

In and of itself a bad idea is manageable: after all, everyone makes them, everyone gets things wrong sometimes. The real problem comes when someone lacks the ability to recognise that their idea is a real stinker. That was the issue in the first decades of the 1900s, when the Australian rules powers that be entertained the idea of merging with rugby league to create a truly national sport. They failed to realise their idea sucked not once, not twice, but three separate times.

The first inkling of it came in 1908, when the Victorian Football League was barely a decade old and the New South Wales Rugby League (NSWRL) was brand spanking new. In that year no lesser a light than rugby league legend Dally Messenger told one of the founders of this new code, J.J. Giltinan, that he should check out Aussie rules. Dally felt the Victorian game had much to offer and that a game that contained the best features of both codes 'would be the most wonderful thing in the world of sport'.

Giltinan travelled to Victoria to sell them on his idea that would soon be tagged 'Universal Football'. 'No doubt you will agree with me that at the present time there is no opening for your game of Australian football – good game though it is – outside your own state of Victoria, South Australia, [Western] Australia and Tasmania,' Giltinan told the footy officials.

Rather than point out that in his own words Giltinan had said Australian football was popular in twice as many states as league and send him packing back to New South Wales, the Victorian league apparently accepted his proposal and passed it onto the national council. 'Both games will benefit but the Australian rules game must be brought into line with the Northern Union game, though of course the latter must also give away something,' Giltinan said. 'There is not such a vast difference between the two [sports].'

Obviously, there would be some changes to the rules of both sports. The version he was selling called for 13 players a side, with the aim of the game being to kick the ball over the crossbar of rugby league–style posts with no behind posts to speak of. The crossbar was a feature because some in Australian rules circles felt goals that rolled in along the ground shouldn't really be considered.

Right off the bat *The Sydney Morning Herald* spotted what went on to become the major hurdle in creating this strange beast of universal football: the offside rule. In Australian rules there was no such thing; players could take possession of the ball from anywhere on the field, which allowed for the already spectacular marking contests. In league, however, any attacking player in front of the ball was deemed to be out of play. 'The rock the movement is likely to split upon from an Australian [rules] standpoint is the suggestion to introduce off-side,' the *Herald* reported. 'If there is one thing the Victorians have no time for it is that.'

Indeed, anything that removed the marking contest was obviously not going to fly with footy fans, but the main impediment to any merger was one of ambition. The Australian Football Council (AFC) wanted to keep their sport within Australia and the universal football hybrid only to be played internationally, a key driver for them being the idea that its players would be able to compete internationally, something not available in a sport played nowhere but Australia. The merger idea sat there for several years until 1914, when none other than Charles Brownlow (the medal guy) compared the crowds drawn by the touring Great Britain Lions matches with those of the Australian rules interstate carnival held in New South Wales for the first time.

Not surprisingly, New South Wales spectators were way more interested in league than Aussie rules. A total of 50,000 spectators watched the 14 carnival games, around 3,500 per match, which didn't look great alongside the 38,000-plus crowds drawn to watch the Lions play Australia. Showing a somewhat naïve approach, Brownlow felt combining the two codes would therefore draw big crowds in both Victoria and New South Wales, and everywhere else in the country.

This time merger talks were a bit more serious, with a series of conferences held between officials of both codes. Of course, they paid little mind to the fact that aside from themselves there was little appetite for universal football from the supporters of either sport. 'The proposed amalgamation, one is afraid, is not taken seriously by anybody outside the immediate officials concerned,' *The Leader* reported. 'There are too many people devoted to the Australian game to allow its being supplanted by a new code, half rugby, half their own.'

The Leader figured those in New South Wales felt the same way: 'We may be quite sure that the rugby league people will never sacrifice their present important international standing to evolve a new game, the effect of which would be to abandon forever those interests.'

Clearly not realising their idea lacked merit, the conference delegates went ahead and devised some rules for this new code. The 13-a-side suggestion of 1908 was changed to 15, playing on a field not more than 146 metres long by 91 metres wide. Points would be scored via a rugby league try or by kicking the ball Aussie rules style between the posts – as long as it went over the crossbar, of course. The centre square bounce would be retained as a way to restart play after a team had scored. The offside rule remained a point of contention. One New South Wales delegate suggested a compromise that was unlikely to work: that the offside rule would only be enforced within the teams' quarters and the centre space would be a free area.

The New South Wales committee that attended the conference was in favour of the amalgamation, but NSWRL secretary Horrie Miller decided his code wouldn't take things further until the Australian rules authorities showed their hand. If they were also in favour there was the likelihood of exhibition matches being played in 1915, with a more serious competition starting as soon as 1916. Victorian clubs such as Melbourne, St Kilda, Geelong, Essendon and Collingwood had ticked off on the rule changes, while Carlton gave the new game cautious approval. However, support was far from unanimous: the *Sunday Times* noted that a handful of rebel Victorian clubs who chose to say no to universal football could start their own competition. No prizes for guessing which code of football the locals would then follow.

The state Australian rules bodies were asked for their input. Some of them opted to make no decision on the new game, a clear indication of their lack of enthusiasm. It wasn't the obvious opposition to the new code that stopped it from going ahead, but World War I. The narrow-minded officials felt that with a war on it might not be the best time to invest heavily in developing a new code and setting up exhibition matches.

A writer for *The Age* with the pseudonym 'Pivot' tried to put the concept back on the agenda in 1919 after the war had ended. He believed that the officials had stymied any chance at growing the game, or at least a version of it, outside of Australia: 'Great sport as the Australian game is – "Australian" is used advisedly – there is not another branch of virile athletics which is so inconsequential in a general sense,' he wrote. 'Its interests are purely local and its progress has been on well-restricted lines.'

No one else was biting. Right there is where the whole rather ludicrous idea should have died, and maybe it would have if the long-serving secretaries of the NSWRL in Miller and the Australian National Football Council's (previously the AFC) Con Hickey hadn't bumped into each other on a boat trip between Melbourne and Sydney in 1933. On that voyage they chose to talk about this universal football idea that both still thought was awesome.

They had further conferences and took another look at the rules. Perhaps to look busy they tinkered further with the rules: the need for a running player to bounce the ball was removed, and Australian rules–style goal squares were added in front of the goalposts at each end of the field. There were even dreams that this new sport they were creating would appeal to the United States – which, to be fair, wasn't as stupid as it sounds. At the time gridiron was on the nose due to occasional fatalities, some of which came from a flying wedge play where the rest of the team lined up behind the ball carrier and propelled him into the teeth of the defence. Sometimes the ball carrier at the point of the wedge didn't survive. The US code was so problematic that President Theodore Roosevelt threatened to abolish the game if changes weren't made.

This third attempt to get universal football off the ground did get one step further than previous attempts: the concept was taken out of the boardroom and onto the field. On 11 August a secret match was held at Sydney's Moore Park, with teams made up of visiting Queensland Aussie rules players supplemented by some local league players. Even so, they couldn't get enough for a 15-a-side match so the trial featured 12 players per side. This hit out included the testing of a way to work around the pesky offside rule, whereby a soccer-style approach would be taken in which a player was onside as long as there were two defenders between him and the goal.

The match wasn't as secret as the universal football proponents might have hoped, because a *Sun* journalist crept inside to watch the game. He was quite gentle in his report, recognising the match was more to familiarise the players with the rules than to convert any observers. He liked the offside approach, saying it allowed players to kick forward 'having the effect of producing the high marks of Australian rules, drawing out defenders to soar into the air with the attacker to get the ball'. The rule that a tackled player had to give the ball to the opposition also got the tick, because it added speed to the game.

Hickey was also impressed with what he saw. 'There is no doubt that if the rules are persevered with something will come out of it,' he told *The Herald*. 'Even though the players who took part knew little or nothing of the rules, there were phases of the play that produced sparkling and brilliant football.' He felt the rugby league style of tackling should become a feature of the new game, as it was better than the Australian rules version. 'When I was an active player with Fitzroy there was tackling in the Australian game, not so pronounced as you have it in rugby. I consider there is a good deal in tackling. It would wipe out a tremendous lot of the free kicks now given in our game.'

While in Sydney to watch this not-so-secret trial match, Hickey took the chance to talk to the Sydney sporting media to sell them on universal football: 'Australian rules is a great game but I realise that such a grand sporting community as we have in every state should be provided with a game with general appeal in the same sense as cricket, lawn tennis and golf possesses. When this matter was discussed in 1914 and we agreed tentatively to give certain rules a trial, we made surprising progress. I believe that if the war had not broken out something definite would have been then attained.'

However, nothing was attained this time around either. The conference created a final draft of the rules and passed them on the various state leagues of the existing codes for future consideration. The NSWRL basically killed the concept by saying 'No, thanks' just a few days later, although the final vote of 15–10 against suggested there was still a sizeable amount of support among the Sydney officials for universal football. Hickey declared disappointment at the NSWRL decision. 'That appears to be the end of it,' he said. 'We can do nothing further.'

The rugby league decision was expected by the leaders of other Australian rules bodies. New South Wales Australian rules league secretary J. Allison wasn't surprised nothing came of the plan, as it was never going to be an easy thing to implement: 'Personally, I do not think there is a hope of making drastic changes,' he said. 'It must be a matter of evolution, and it will take a matter of 10 years of hard work and hard thinking to get over the matter.'

His Australian Rules league president A. Provan wasn't surprised either. He expected the league to say no. 'Personally I think it was the only natural result,' he said. 'It was obviously too hard for either code to give away so much to make it practical. But I will say this – if anyone will be the loser it will be the NSWRL.'

10

THE DANGERS OF GOLF

If they had it their way the vast majority of footy players would want to play forever, but that's not a possibility: age and injury or a combination of both will inevitably force them into retirement whether they want to or not. For the most part injuries are caused by some on-field collision or a sudden movement in a certain direction that caused the knee ligaments to say 'Nope, not doing that.' What no player expects is to have the curtains pulled down on their career thanks to a golf cart, but that's just what happened to Bulldogs legend Brad Johnson in the 2010 season. The smiling 182-centimetre forward debuted for the Dogs in round 18 of 1994, a 32-point win over Collingwood. He became a long-time Dog, breaking Chris Grant's 341-game club record in a 2009 match against Fremantle – coincidentally in the same round that he made his debut.

By the time the 2010 season rolled around Johnson was 33 years old and starting to feel the effects of injury and age. Johnson had missed the entire NAB Cup pre-season tournament with a calf injury but managed to make it on the field for the round 1 match against Collingwood, in which the Magpies thumped them by 36 points. He'd pulled up a bit sore after that game and was on light duties at training when the bizarre incident with the golf cart happened. Johnson was having a kick to kick with Grant when property steward Noel Kinniburgh drove the cart at low speed into Johnson's calf, the very same one that had caused him to sit out the pre-season.

The incident was captured by the Fox TV cameras and is still available online. While Dogs coach Rodney 'Rocket' Eade seemed keen to downplay the whole thing as nothing but a bit of fun, even to the point where making jokes at Kinniburgh's expense seemed to be his focus, Johnson didn't seem happy when he hobbled off the field. As Eade told radio station SEN: 'The poor old bloke that drove the cart is having kittens at the moment. He's in a state of depression because as you would know at a footy club the players haven't let him off lightly. Noel didn't think anything of it because he didn't have any speed up and then Brad went in [to the rooms] to get checked out.

'Everyone was into Noel, saying "You've wrecked his career, he's not going to play again" and "He's out this week" and "What are you doing?" Poor old Noel is in a state of depression and he's gone home sick.'

Eade told the AFL website that Johnson was fine and would play on the weekend. 'It was quite funny in the end,' he said. 'It was serious to start with but he's okay and there's no drama with it.' However, Johnson didn't play in round 2 against Richmond, with the blame going to a virus – though the media intimated that the golf cart incident was also a factor. He then missed round 3 at home against Hawthorn and round 4 against

Brisbane. He didn't make it back onto the field until the round 5 away match against Adelaide. 'I haven't had the best start in regards to injury, the virus and a few other things,' Johnson said in the *Herald Sun*. 'Hopefully now I can get on with the season.'

Johnson played two games in a row and then was out of the side for the round 7 meeting with Melbourne and didn't return until round 13. All up he played 15 games in the 2010 season: the only time he played fewer games in his 17-year career was his debut season, when he made it onto the field nine times.

The stop-start nature of his season led to Johnson announcing his retirement on 6 September, and he played his last game for the Western Bulldogs in the preliminary final loss to St Kilda two weeks later. After Johnson's retirement was announced his manager, Ricky Nixon, came out and suggested the golf cart had hastened the end of his client's career: 'I don't want to create something out of nothing here,' he said in the *Herald Sun*, 'but I think you'll find that it was a little bit worse than what it was, as in, it was made out to be a bit of a tap and a bit of a joke and everything else, but I don't think it was quite as simple.'

Johnson went on to have a career as a commentator and pundit with Fox Footy, where the golf cart is brought up several times a year. While he admitted in 2020 that he could see the funny side of it, there was nothing to laugh about at the time. As he told the *Herald Sun*: 'I was just having some shots at goal and doing my own thing after training had just about finished and the whistle blew and I got hit. I didn't actually get hit that hard by the golf cart. It was just unfortunately the box underneath it that clipped my Achilles and I had a bad Achilles.

It just blew up instantly. So I was out of the game for a month for being hit by a golf cart. Who decided to bring golf carts onto the footy field anyway?'

Incidentally, it's not the only golfing-related injury that put a player on the sidelines. On a day off in 2021 St Kilda's Max King was playing a round of golf on a course with friends in the Melbourne suburb of Brighton. Somehow during the round King copped a golf ball to the head, and later tests by the club found he had suffered a mild concussion. Under the AFL's new rules a player couldn't take the field for 12 days after suffering a concussion, so even though King's injury happened on the golf course rather than the playing field he had to sit out the Saints' season opener against the Giants.

11

A LOW-SCORING DECIDER

A final score line of 25–13 sounds like something from a rugby league match, not a football game, and certainly not a footy match that decided the premiers – yet it did. It gets even weirder: there wasn't a single goal scored in the first quarter. The two sides went into the quarter-time break with the scores 0.4 (4) to 0.1 (1). The teams in this weirdest of weird matches that decided the 1927 competition were Collingwood and Richmond. The former was up four points to one after that ridiculously low-scoring first quarter, but the Collingwood side came back to take the match 2.13 (25) to 1.7 (13).

The pressing question is: how do the top two teams in the 1927 season fail to even crack the half-century when both their scores are combined? Well, to put it bluntly, it absolutely pissed down. The rain started at 2.00 pm on game day and was still pelting down when the match started at 3.00 pm. 'Footballers slithered about as if on a skating rink and cut some queer capers,' the *Geelong Advertiser* stated. 'The ground gradually became a quagmire and players found it almost impossible to keep their feet.'

The *Sporting Globe* branded it a 'dreary, dismal day for football' and also used the ice-skating reference: 'The condition of the turf would have suited an aquatic carnival more than football. Had the ground been frozen, ice skating would have been better to the liking of the crowd.'

In Monday's *Herald* football writer 'Kickero' ridiculed the decision of the league to go ahead with the game: 'As a spectacle it was amusing at times but as for football, and football to decide the great premiership issue, it was a dismal failure.' He noted the charmingly named 'inclement weather committee' had until noon to postpone a footy match; after that time it must go ahead.

Perhaps foreseeing the future AFL and its belief to be a power unto itself, Kickero felt the league should have ignored the rules: 'The league is more powerful than any of its committees and the first clause of its constitution states that it can do any act or deed in the interests of the game. Surely it was in the interests of the game and of the people who keep it going – the great paying public – to have postponed the match. The sooner the league grasps this phase of the question the better.'

The game itself was obviously not that impressive, though a frankly astonishing 34,551 people braved the rain to sit in the stands and watch. With the centre square a mud patch and pools of water along the wings, there was nowhere that a player could find a safe patch of grass. Much of the kicking was done off the ground, with players realising the ball was the proverbial cake of soap and couldn't be picked up.

The players seemed frustrated by the difficult conditions and spent just as much time bashing each other up as trying to score.

As recorded in *The Argus*: 'Throughout the match considerable bitterness was displayed between the various players. It is difficult to say how it began – it was probably an aftermath of previous meetings – but very early in the game blows were exchanged between several opponents. One of the Collingwood players concerned received a rough handling all through the game but it cannot be said that he turned the other cheek.'

At half-time the players took the unusual step of changing into fresh, dry jerseys although Richmond might not have brought enough replacements, because one newspaper reported the side returned to the field in 'a pie-bald appearance, some being in red and white jerseys, others blue and white and others again showing even greater variety'.

The fans had come to see whether Collingwood superboot Gordon Coventry would crack the ton. He woke up that morning on 95 goals and it seemed a sure thing that he'd get another five in the final, but the rain had other ideas: Coventry managed just two goals, both in the second quarter. Richmond didn't goal until the final quarter.

Overall, Collingwood won the very muddy affair because it better adapted to the conditions. 'Collingwood displayed better tactics, particularly in regard to long kicking whenever the ball was picked up,' *The Argus* wrote. 'It showed a greater pertinacity and also handled the ball better, while the players were content to stand down and allow Richmond to fly for and miss the ball. Richmond on the other hand, while showing greater dash, tried to pick up the ball too often instead of kicking along the ground. While goals were usually a matter of good fortune, Richmond missed more easy chances than did Collingwood.'

The win ended a period of disappointment for Collingwood, who had lost grand finals in 1920, 1922, 1925 and 1926. That 1927 season sparked a golden period for the club where it won four straight flags, which is still a record, and saw the side nicknamed 'The Machine'. The 1929 side managed the impressive feat of going through the season undefeated, though in 1927 captain Syd Coventry – Gordon's brother, appointed to the position just that season after the club had sacked in-form leader Charlie Tyson – didn't seem in the mood to celebrate the grand final win. One match report said Coventry fought his team-mates' attempt to chair him off the ground and struggled to be put back down.

The drama of the decider didn't end with the full-time siren, when a fan had another supporter charged with assault over an incident that started in the grandstand. Robert Andrews claimed in court he was sitting with his friend Eddie Norton and turned to him and said: 'By the look of things it's 10 to one to Richmond.' According to Andrews, it was then that John Otten punched him in the eye. Andrews said he tried to get a policeman to arrest Otten, only to be told to let it go. After the match Andrews said he sought out Otten, shook hands and had a few beers. He later found himself on the same tram as Otten and must have changed his mind, because when Otten got off Andrews followed him, found a policeman and had Otten charged.

Otten told the court a very different story indeed, saying Andrews had been shouting '10 to one to Richmond' in his ear. Otten told him to go and bother someone else and said he hadn't struck Andrews, merely pushed him. A witness in court supported Otten's testimony, while a police officer said Otten was drunk. However, the judge mustn't have believed Andrews because he dismissed the case.

Another piece of drama was created by Collingwood treasurer R.T. Rush. Immediately after Collingwood's win Rush must have been feeling generous, because he suggested the two teams should come back the following Saturday and stage a charity match. Several people took what was possibly an off-the-cuff suggestion to heart and began organising it. The lord mayor decided his charity would be the one to get the money and the charity's secretary got to work getting the consent of the league, access to the Melbourne Cricket Ground (MCG), the umpires and the Richmond club's agreement to play the game. All that was left was the formal assent of the Collingwood board.

They said 'No', while perhaps silently cursing Rush and his big mouth. To be fair to Collingwood they had nothing to gain and everything to lose: if they played the game and lost then it would be suggestive that they weren't the true premiers. Instead, they said they were willing to play a team drawn from all the league sides, which didn't work as far as the league was concerned because all the other teams had ceased training a few weeks earlier and wouldn't be match fit. Thus the charity match suggested by a Collingwood official didn't happen because Collingwood said 'No'.

The biggest news broke more than three weeks after the final, but it didn't relate to the final. Instead, it was about a confrontation that occurred outside the MCG after the Richmond–Carlton semi-final on 17 September. One of the participants was Richmond's George Rudolph, who had once been spotted smoking on the field during a 1925 match where Richmond took on a New South Wales side. While holding the cigarette in one hand he took a mark with the other, then turned sharply towards the goal and knocked the umpire out cold in the process. After he goaled he put the ciggie in his mouth and bent down to pick up the umpire.

The other participant in the 1927 incident was North Melbourne's Johnny Lewis. Before the league tribunal Rudolph said he was leaving the ground in the company of his fiancée and her friend when Lewis approached him out of an alleyway, calling the Richmond player a 'mug footballer'. Tigers vice president Harry Dyke was following behind; Lewis took a swing at Rudolph, who ducked it, and the punch ended up connecting with Dyke.

Rudolph handed his hat and bag to the ladies and waded into Lewis. They grappled for a few minutes before Rudolph fell to the ground and was kicked a few times. Lewis wasn't the sort of man you'd want to take on in a fight: at 99 kilograms and 191 centimetres tall he was reportedly the biggest man in the league at the time, so Rudolph was giving up 7 kilos and 6 centimetres in height to his rival. The brawl had ended when police arrived but, curiously, Rudolph insisted to them that he had not been assaulted. In his defence Lewis admitted to verbally abusing Rudolph but insisted he hadn't hit anyone. Yes, he'd had a few drinks beforehand but reckoned he was still able to remember what had happened. The tribunal didn't agree, suspending Lewis for the entire 1928 season.

Oddly enough, it wasn't the only time that year an opponent in a fight with Rudolph had been suspended. During the round 17 Richmond–Carlton fixture Rudolph called Carlton's Frank Irwin 'vile and offensive names'. In retaliation Irwin cracked Rudolph on the jaw and knocked him down. The goal umpire saw it and reported Irwin, and the league tribunal ousted him for 12 months.

SHE HEARD THE VOICES, HEARD THEIR WORDS FROM THE FIRST TIME SHE STEPPED ON THE FIELD . . .

12

STANDING UP

She heard the voices, heard their words from the first time she stepped on the field for the Aspley Hornets' under-six side. It's where she wanted to be from the first moment she saw her older brother Jack running around with the Hornets' under sevens. As the only girl in the team, the only girl on the field, she stood out and that made her a target for hurtful, unnecessary words from the sidelines from grown-ups who you'd expect would know better: telling her she shouldn't be playing, that she lacked the skills, that she should leave it to the boys. When that happened the girl would go tackle their son as hard as she could.

There were the comments from the boys on the other side as well, either whingeing because they thought they'd have to go easy on her or gloating that they were going to smash her. Funnily enough, that's just what she wanted. 'I would grab the footy and either no one would touch me and let me go through,' she told *Stellar* magazine, 'or they would annihilate me, which was my preferred option because I just wanted to be treated like everyone else.'

The girl who would soon make it impossible to be treated like everyone else in the local comps was Tayla Harris. She went through with the boys up to the under 14s comp, when she was told she couldn't be a part of the team. At the age of just 14 she earned a spot in the Queensland women's under-18s side, then a year later she was named the best and fairest player in Queensland's top competition.

Harris was destined for bigger and better things, so at the age of 17 she was drafted by Melbourne for a series of women's AFL exhibition matches. In 2017 she was back in her home state as the marquee signing for the Brisbane Lions AFL Women's (AFLW) side, then to Carlton in 2017 and back to Melbourne for the 2022 season. Along the way she was nominated for the Rising Star Award, made the All-Australian team four times, was three-time leading goal scorer for Carlton and topped the goal-scoring list in her first season back with Melbourne in 2022. Oh, and she also tried her hand at boxing, starting in 2017 when she won seven of her first eight fights, three of them by knockout. The other one was a draw, not a loss, in case you're wondering.

In 2019 Harris hit the headlines after being photographed kicking the first goal in Carlton's match against the Western Bulldogs, where the Blues held on to win 6.5 (41) to 5.8 (38). Michael Willson's photograph caught her in her follow-through: she'd gotten some air so it looks as though she's hovering over the ground, right leg extended so her foot is above her head and her left arm crosses over that leg at the shin. In some ways it wasn't anything new: Google will throw up any number of photos showing Harris's distinctive, long-limbed kicking style. One of them, taken by photographer Michael Dodge just two rounds earlier, is an almost identical shot but from the opposite angle.

What was different about Willson's photo was that the Seven Network chose to post it to their 7AFL Facebook page, after which the trolls showed their true colours by posting some ugly comments. Sadly, the comments were far from unusual: female rights group Plan International studied Facebook comments left on a variety of pages, including those of various TV sports shows, and found more than one quarter of the comments about female players were negative compared with just 9 per cent for men. Unlike the sportsmen, a chunk of the comments sexualised sportswomen and belittled their abilities in comparison with the men's league, as though the players weren't aware there was a difference in skill level between the AFL and the AFLW.

'I know there are comments about women's football,' Geelong ruck Erin Hoare said to *The Age* the week Harris's photo was posted. 'We're not blind to [what we] produce, we understand what our game looks like, but we have to understand where we've come from and the lack of opportunity that's existed and how extraordinary that we are where we are now and where we're going to be.' All the pathways to the top level of football have been there for men for ages, but for women . . . well, those opportunities are just starting to appear. To criticise the standard of play at AFLW falsely assumes players in both competitions had the same advantages when they didn't.

As far as the Harris photo goes, the whole thing didn't really kick off until someone looking after the Seven Network's Facebook page got nervous and took the picture down. 'The image attracted a number of comments, some of which were inappropriate and offensive,' a statement from the Seven

Network read. 'As a consequence we have removed the image and the comments.' The outrage about Seven's actions on social media is perhaps best summed up by Matildas' player Sam Kerr, who pressed caps lock and wrote: 'THE PROBLEM WAS NOT THE PHOTO'.

It wasn't the only photo of an AFLW player removed from a Facebook page and it wasn't the only post removed that weekend. Collingwood's Cecilia McIntosh, a Commonwealth Games silver medallist in javelin and Australian Olympian in bobsled, had played her last game that weekend and a photo of her being chaired off the field was removed from another footy Facebook page due to unsavoury comments that were posted. One of those was from a former male AFL player who mocked her for playing 'gruelling' eight-match seasons for three years.

AFL boss Gillon McLachlan was seemingly not quite as supportive of Harris as many others, saying in *The Australian*: 'These things happen and people do their best to monitor them, but in the end self-regulation and accountability is what needs to happen here and that is what's happening . . . It's a big wide world out there and you can't do it all. So there's broader accountability by the public.' Keep in mind that a number of the offending comments would have come from supporters of the men's game and that maybe it was the right time to send a message to the trolls.

Within five hours of removing the image the Seven Network issued a mea culpa, saying it would 'work harder to ban trolls from our pages', and reposted it. It was actually the removal of the photo that had highlighted the issue of sexist comments and perhaps showed the trolls that there could be repercussions to their ill-thought-out comments. A few months later Harris told *Stellar* she understood the situation the 7AFL moderators were in: 'Some people have interpreted Seven's move as not supporting women but I don't think 7AFL were doing it maliciously, and I'm sure they would have done it differently if they knew what was going to unfold after.'

In the space between when the post was pulled down and then reposted Harris went on the front foot, posting it to her own social media with the caption: 'Here's a pic of me at work . . . think about this before your derogatory comments, animals.' However, there was understandable fear behind the brave stance. As Harris said in *The Canberra Times*: 'These people are behind screens now but no one's saying they aren't going to show up at the footy this weekend. How do I identify if that was the person who made this comment directed at me, because now I'm uncomfortable in my workspace. [W]hat are they going to do when I'm on the sideline meeting some kids: that's what I'm going to have to think about now.'

At the preliminary final her Carlton side booked a place in the grand final with a 36-point win over Fremantle. There was still a wave of support for Harris: before the match the AFL handed out badges showing a silhouette of Harris's kick, but days later the AFL took another backwards step when they threatened legal action against T-shirt company League Tees for releasing a shirt with a design inspired by the photo of Harris. The league claimed it was a 'substantial reproduction' of an image owned by them.

League Tees owner and designer Anthony Costa pulled the shirts, but he told *The Age* he wasn't happy: 'It's an original, it took a bloody long time for us to draw it and get it right. People loved it, it's raised a lot of money for a really important charity [the Australian Literacy and Numeracy Foundation]. It's something we're proud to have been involved with.'

Greg Baum, sportswriter for *The Age*, criticised the AFL's approach as being more focused on the brand than the bigger issue: 'This is what the AFL willfully overlooks in claiming ownership. It is a mistake it makes too often to be accidental. It confuses the business, which it does own, with the game, which it patently does not.'

The photo won an award at the inaugural Women in Sport Photo Action Awards and was turned into a bronze statue that was unveiled in Federation Square before finding a permanent home at Docklands. 'We're committed to celebrating the incredible achievements of more women through our public monuments,' Melbourne's lord mayor Sally Capp said, 'providing inspiration for young Melburnians while spreading awareness of our diverse role models.'

A few months later Harris reflected in *Stellar* on what had happened in the wake of the photo being posted online: 'I am glad it unfolded how it did; it's been positive. The message has been read, the conversation started. It should have been sooner but it's happening now, and every move is forward now in my view.'

13

FOOTY AT THE OLYMPICS

The 1956 grand final didn't impress the Melbourne Olympic organising committee. It wasn't the score line that upset them, unless some of them were Collingwood fans. The Demons took out their second straight flag with an absolute shellacking of the Magpies 17.19 (121) to 6.12 (48). Collingwood must have thought they were in with a chance early, leading by 5 after the first quarter and then facing a 20-point gap at the long break. From there the Demons poured it on, scoring 73 second-half points to the Magpies' 21.

The Melbourne Cricket Ground (MCG) had been altered to try to fit in large crowds, but the changes weren't anywhere near enough to squeeze in all those who wanted to see the grand final. The official crowd was a then-record 115,802; there was so little space in the stands that people were standing in the aisles, which led *The Argus* to report that people seated in those stands couldn't get down the stairs to go to the toilets. Kids jumped the fence and sat on the grass close to the boundary, leading to a number of players crashing into them. *The Argus* ran a photo showing Collingwood's Bob Kupsch pulling up right at the first row, though momentum must have surely carried him further into the rows of kids.

The goings-on outside the ground as fans tried to get in after the gates were closed put fear into the Olympic body. Using their most outraged capitals, *The Argus* titled their article 'A NATIONAL DISGRACE': 'It was an exhibition of rioting and official bungling that has caused a near panic in Olympic Games circles,' the paper wrote.

Fans climbed the high walls and sat on top of them or on the roof of the old stand. Those outside smashed their bodies into the closed gates, desperate to force their way into the ground; estimates were that around 2,500 were successful. A heavy steel shutter was lifted and buckled so that people could crawl underneath it, while elsewhere others scaled a spiked fence, raced across the Melbourne Cricket Club (MCC) bowling green and then climbed another fence to get into the MCG.

'Outside the ground, after the Health Department ordered the gates closed it was like a Hollywood version of the storming of the Bastille,' stated *The Argus*. 'Women and children were knocked over in the rush and a uniformed attendant, Mr J Dunk, was punched in the face.'

The chief executive officer of the Olympic committee, Lieutenant General Sir William Bridgeford, said they were expecting around 110,000 for the opening ceremony in around two months' time and the grand final shenanigans were a worry. 'Maybe what happened at the MCG on Saturday was just as well. It is a warning of what could happen to us on November 22.' He added that if the Olympic crowds were going to behave that way the committee might have to call in the military to keep order.

As an aside, the RSPCA wasn't pleased with the grand final either. At one stage in the game a Collingwood supporter released several magpies, some of which had had their wings clipped so they landed on the playing field. The RSPCA's chief inspector, A.M. Hendry was most unhappy: 'The birds are protected,' he said in *The Argus*, 'and it was sheer cruelty to clip their wings and throw them on the ground.' Collingwood secretary Gordon Carlyon was also not amused, telling *The Argus*: 'The magpie is our emblem and we hated to see it misused in this way.'

While the Olympic committee was displeased with the grand final shenanigans, it wasn't enough to see them run a red line through plans to have Australian rules at the Melbourne Games. The host city always gets to pick two demonstration sports, one national sport and one foreign to the hosts. It led to some unusual decisions in the past: in 1900 the Paris body opted for pigeon racing, and London in 1904 thought bicycle polo was a great idea. No, I'm not making that up; apparently bicycle polo was enough of a thing that they even held an international tournament seven years earlier.

The Melbourne committee chose football in July 1954, and some months later as the foreign sport they chose baseball. One obvious hiccup was the Olympic ideal of the amateur athlete: with the VFL allowing players to be paid, a good many of them were ruled out of selection. However, the rules seemed to have been bent somewhat to allow those players who weren't solely reliant on footy payments to play in the game. All players would be required to sign a declaration that they weren't professionals.

Ruling out professional footballers meant having two recognisable VFL teams playing at the Games wouldn't work, so two representative teams were chosen. Even then it seems as though they weren't able to find enough decent amateur VFL players to fill a side, so one of the teams was a combination of players from the VFL and the Victorian Football Association (VFA). The other side was made up of representatives from the Victorian Amateur Football Association (VAFA).

Despite payments being allowed decades earlier, there were still some amateurs in the VFL: Richmond's Vic Naismith also competed in the javelin at athletics events and kept his amateur status while the captain of the VFL–VFA side, Denis Cordner, came from a long family line of players who didn't play for money. Other VFL players who made the cut included Collingwood's Ray Gabelich and Brian Gray, Footscray's John Westacott and Brendan Edwards of Hawthorn. As an emergency sub a VFA player by the name of Linsday Gaze was named (Andrew Gaze's father). Gaze didn't get on the field, and two years later he gave up footy in preference to basketball.

The match was scheduled to take place on the second last day of the Games after the bronze medal soccer match between Bulgaria and India, which Bulgaria won 3–0. The estimated attendance for the afternoon session was 36,200, but if footage of the exhibition match is any indication then around 35,000 of those people left after Bulgaria's bronze. The two sides were decked out in long-sleeved jerseys: the VAFA's were white with green collars, cuffs and numbers, while the VFL–VFA's jerseys were green with a white trim. Both had the Olympic rings embroidered on the chest.

With the footy only a demonstration sport, not much in the way was done to accommodate it on the field. Pits for the long jump and other events were filled in and the cinder running track around the stadium was left in place. VAFA defender Tony Capes remembered playing on the running track: 'The 10-yard square was marked out on the cinders,' he told the *AFL Record*. 'As I kicked the drop kick, my toe dug into the track and I almost broke my foot.'

Brian Gray was on the flank and spent most of his game running along the track. 'What I recall more than anything else was playing on the half-forward flank and running up and down on the cinder track, which was still there and not covered,' he told the *Football Record*. 'I don't think anyone cared about it. We were just happy to be out there.'

The most unexpected obstacle was a flagpole flying the Olympic rings flag: it couldn't be removed, so the boundary line for the match had to snake around it. VFL–VFA player Des Tobin remembered that damned flagpole for the *Record*: 'You'd come flying down the MCC members' wing and the boundary line jutted out and around the flag pole,' he said. 'The official Olympic flag was at full mast. It couldn't come down until the closing ceremony.'

The VFL–VFA team suffered for not having a recognised goal kicker, with the VAFA running out winners 12.9 (81) to 8.7 (55). 'The Victorian amateur team won, won well, and deserved the victory,' wrote *The Argus*'s Percy Taylor. 'It was a better combination, it shone in the air, it fumbled rarely, and it seemed the faster. The combined VFL–VFA team had some good individual players, but there was an absence of punch in their play.'

The game meant a lot to some of the players, all of whom were given a bronze participant's medal, and particularly Dick Fenton-Smith, who was named best on ground. Not only had he represented his country at the Olympics, it would fast track his move to the VFL. He was added to the seniors training list at Melbourne in 1957 and played for three seasons, making the decider in each year and winning two of them.

One opinion is that the spectators were left less than impressed, and perhaps bewildered, by what they had seen: As Percy Taylor wrote: 'If my guess is right, they were not tremendously impressed. Let me hasten to say no one should be really surprised they gained that impression. Why? It was out of season, which is fatal. It was an exhibition and, as such, lacked the fire that makes our game. And there was the absence of that partisan spirit, the life blood of our game.'

The reporter for *The Age* noted the perplexed reaction to the goal umpires, with one spectator turning in his seat to ask the journo: 'What gives with the guys in the white butcher's coats?' Jim Dunaway from Chicago, however, was impressed by one aspect of the game: 'The player's kicking ability, both for distance and accuracy has amazed me. I thoroughly enjoyed it.'

The official report of the Organising Committee for the Games saw the match this way: 'The game was played in the true amateur spirit, with [an] abundance of vigour and speed, plenty of good kicking and high marking, system and other characteristics of Australian football. The spectator participation which as outspoken "barracking" is such a marked feature of the game in Australia was missing; this was to be expected, perhaps, as the game was played not so much to spectators of this kind as to overseas visitors, to demonstrate the finer points of the game.

'The demonstration, as such, did not suffer a whit from this lack of the traditional Saturday atmosphere; it was soundly played, all members of the teams acquitting themselves with honour.'

One advantage of the match was that it hastened the televising of football. Having the Olympics broadcast offered up a trial run to see if football could be made to work on television. The match wasn't shown live but on a closed circuit, so if it didn't work no one would see it. With sport on television being very new because television itself was very new, overseas experts looked at the size of the field and figured it couldn't be done, but Alf Potter and Gordon Bennett, who were in charge of the Olympic coverage, used quick cuts and sharp camerawork to make things interesting.

When football's powerbrokers saw the result they were less than impressed: 'They dismissed the broadcast's potential almost out of hand, fearful that a superior television product would harm gate receipts,' *The Guardian*'s Russell Jackson wrote. League president Kenneth Luke said it wasn't practical at the moment, but the league soon changed their tune and gave the Seven and Nine networks and the ABC the rights to televise the last quarter of the same live game each week. In return, each paid £3,000.

On 20 April 1957 those people with television sets or who knew a neighbour who had one sat in front of them at 4.15 pm to watch the final quarter of the round 1 Essendon–Collingwood match held at Victoria Park over the Easter weekend. There had been plans for each station to show a different match, with program guides stating Nine Network had Essendon–Collingwood, the ABC got Carlton–Hawthorn and the Seven Network would screen the Saints versus the Swans.

However, that changed on the morning of the games: a front-page story in *The Age* said there was a disagreement between the VFL and the body known as the Grounds Management Association over payment. As Victoria Park was the only venue not part of that association, televising the Essendon–Collingwood match was free to go ahead. On the Easter Monday the Nine Network also screened the Geelong–Footscray match at Kardinia Park, another venue not part of the Grounds Management Association.

Television and footy were strange bedfellows for some time. After crowds began to decline slightly between 1957 and 1960 the VFL decided television was to blame and refused a request from the networks to extend the last-quarter coverage. It wasn't until the mid-1970s that footy returned to television on a weekly basis.

The 1961 grand final was allowed to be televised, on delay, but only after all the tickets had been sold. Grand finals weren't shown live until 1977. That match ended in a draw between

North Melbourne and Collingwood, so fans got to see two grand finals on television that year. Of course, these days the AFL is more than happy to let the games appear on television because of the millions and millions of dollars the networks pay for the privilege.

DURING THE THREE-QUARTER HUDDLE CAPTAIN CONDON, DRESSED IN HIS CIVVIES, CAME TO BLOWS WITH TEAM-MATE ARTHUR ROBSON . . .

14

CONDON'S CHAOS

No doubt about it: Dick Condon was a great player. The *Encyclopedia of AFL Footballers* goes further, suggesting he 'was probably the greatest player of his era'. He was possibly also the crankiest. To say he had a short fuse would be misleading, as it implies there was some length of fuse in the first place.

Playing for Collingwood from 1897 to 1900 and again from 1902 to 1906 before a forced move to Richmond in 1908, Condon was the sort of player who lashed out at team-mates, officials and umpires, leaving the impression that he failed to grasp it might be him and not everyone else who was wrong. It is a telling sign that Collingwood didn't award him life membership until 2013, waiting for him to be dead for 67 years lest he blow up at the presentation night.

The season that best exhibits the dark side of Dick was in 1900, when the red mist seemed to descend with regularity. He was so incensed with umpire William Freame during a round 10 match played against South Melbourne on 7 July that he spent much of his time telling the umpire how terrible he was. The league took a dim view of that behaviour, especially coming from a club captain, and suspended Condon for three matches.

However, Condon didn't need to be playing to cause a problem. The following week Collingwood played a severely depleted Essendon side missing at least nine players. According to *The Argus* it looked like the Same Olds might not even be able to find 18 men to put on the field, with the situation being so dire that club secretary William Crebbin had to suit up. He had played for Essendon in the pre-VFL era but hadn't had a game since his retirement in 1896, hence his playing record sits at one VFL/AFL match.

For that reason *The Argus* wasn't too excited about Collingwood's 21-point win: 'The game itself does not require much description, for Collingwood evidently thinking they had an easy task at hand, did not play up to form.' Luckily for *The Argus*, Condon was on hand to liven things up. During the three-quarter huddle captain Condon, dressed in his civvies, came to blows with team-mate Arthur Robson, forcing umpire Freame to separate them.

In the match report *The Argus* saw fit to state the bleeding obvious: 'There is a good deal of growling going on in the Magpies' nest just now, and though the band in the dressing room after the game played patriotic and other airs, there seemed to be several discords in the harmony of the team.' That'll happen when your suspended captain punches a team-mate on the field.

Condon wasn't done just yet. On 1 September in the second sectional round, which were used in lieu of finals to sort out the minor premiers, against Geelong, Condon was so unimpressed with umpire Dick Gibson that he left the field to talk the committee into taking his team off. The committee said 'No' and the papers felt Condon was over-reacting: Gibson wasn't cheating, he was just terrible. 'Even from a Geelong point of view, he was not a success,' stated *The Age* of Gibson. 'It was not that he was partial, but he seemed inefficient.'

The following weekend Condon came up against a truly Crapp umpire: Ivo Crapp. He was actually highly respected, tagged the Prince of Umpires at one stage, and had probably heard every variation of joke someone could come up with in relation to his surname. Condon had been giving Crapp crap since the match had begun, but he took a great big leap over the line when he said: 'Your girl's a bloody whore!' Some suggest Condon was talking about Crapp's daughter but Crapp only had two sons at the time of the slur, so the target was obviously Crapp's wife Priscilla. It should also be noted that no contemporary newspapers record whether this was actually what Condon said, and later references to Condon's slur fail to identify the source.

It's still a good story, though, so let's go with it. Not surprisingly, Crapp took issue with his wife being insulted like that and reported Condon to the league. The league was similarly unimpressed and banned the Collingwood captain for life. In writing of the decision the *Geelong Advertiser* noted the kids of the day might think the penalty for strong language was too severe, but felt the league should be commended for its courage: 'If the game is not to degenerate into an exhibition of brutality and savagery, such conduct must be suppressed with a strong hand. Players must control their temper, sorely as it must often be tried, and the abuse and attempted browbeating of an umpire is an offence which, when sheeted home, must be sharply and severely punished.'

In league terms 'life' evidently meant one year, because after several appeals Condon was back in Collingwood colours for round 2 of the 1902 season. What was going through the heads of his Magpies team-mates in the sheds before that match against Melbourne wasn't recorded, though one assumes they all avoided making eye contact in case it encouraged Condon to whack them.

The returned Collingwood player seemed to behave himself a bit better, with the Magpies taking out the flag that year – in a match umpired by one Ivo Crapp – though Condon hadn't totally changed his stripes: by 1906 the unbelievably patient Collingwood board decided to give him his marching orders. He spent the 1907 season in Tasmania where, in a huge irony, he served as an umpire. On his return to Melbourne he took up the captain–coach role at Richmond, only to ruffle too many feathers and get the chop at the end of the 1909 season.

By 1915 Condon found himself in Sydney, where in August he penned a long letter to *The Referee* outlining what was expected of football players. In it Condon showed he still wasn't one for introspection; as he preached: 'Some players stand many bumps and never attempt to retaliate. Such men do credit to the game and themselves; while others, with little provocation, lose their heads and resort to many things not in the rules.'

If you thought a little self-reflection from Condon would follow you'd be sorely mistaken: he was actually talking about *other* players, not himself: 'To those men I say it is time for coolness. Try to think before you act. Do not bring discredit on yourself and after all is over you will feel contented and retain the respect of your club and comrades' desire. I know it is British pluck to defend oneself but retaliation on the field brings condemnation and stigma.'

If Ivo Crapp and any number of former team-mates and officials read Condon's words they likely would have shaken their heads in amazement.

IT'S THE FIRST VERSE INSPIRED BY THE VIEW OUT HIS WINDOW THAT LEADS PEOPLE TO IDENTIFY IT AS A FOOTY SONG.

15

KELLY COUNTRY

Paul Kelly is an AFL legend. A player with the Sydney Swans for 12 years, he made his debut in 1990 and ended up as captain just three years later. Kelly nabbed the Brownlow in 1995, then a year later he led the Swans to their first grand final since 1945's bloodbath. North beat them by 43 points, and the club had to wait until 2005 for its next flag.

However, this chapter is about another Paul Kelly, one who never played a single VFL or AFL match but managed to be on the hallowed turf of the Melbourne Cricket Ground (MCG) on grand final day twice – with a guitar rather than a Sherrin. The first time was in 2012, coincidentally when the other Kelly's Swans won the decider, and the second in 2019 when the Tigers annihilated Greater Western Sydney.

One song that got an airing on the turf at the G wasn't inspired by footy at all, but in an illustration of how listeners get to decide for themselves what a song means plenty of people have decided that's *exactly* what it's about.

'Leaps and Bounds' had been partially written by Kelly and friend Chris Langham back in 1977. At the time it was just a chorus and a melody, and it wasn't until a while later when Kelly moved to a flat in Punt Road in 1980 that he added a few verses with the words 'still about nothing in particular'. It's the first verse inspired by the view out his window that leads people to identify it as a footy song. 'I was living in a first-floor flat and out my window I could see the Nylex clock and the MCG,' Kelly told magazine *The Music*, 'so that's where that lyric came from. It was never written as a football song, but it's sort of been picked up.'

The song wasn't recorded until 1986, when it appeared on the Paul Kelly and the Coloured Girls' double album *Gossip*. A year later it was released as a single, backed by a song that had obvious sporting inspiration in 'Bradman'. The song 'Leaps and Bounds' was released with a video shot on top of the silos on Punt Road, where the Nylex clock once sat. It was shot in the middle of summer with the temperature in the low 30s but the band is rugged up in jeans, jackets and scarves to fit in with the autumn theme of the song.

Kelly said in his autobiography *How to Make Gravy* it's a song that always seems to get a run in relation to big sporting events, including the AFL grand final. 'That's the song the producers always ask for. It's a proven performer, comes into its own around finals time. Not bad for a song about nothing.'

Kelly has had a long connection with the footy. He had been born in Adelaide into a family that supported the Norwood Redlegs, who still play in the South Australian National Football League (SANFL), back when the VFL hadn't let in any interstate teams. In his autobiography he wrote of the bout of nerves he'd get as a kid while listening to a close game on the radio. In the last quarter he'd turn off the radio, go into the backyard for a quick kick of the footy and then return for a score update. One season when the Redlegs missed out on the finals by a goal, Kelly went to sleep believing the score would be reviewed and he'd wake up the next day to find Norwood had made it through. When he woke up on Sunday morning he raced out to the front yard to get the paper, only to find the Redlegs' fate had not changed. He wouldn't be the only footy fan who had hoped divine intervention would address a terrible wrong that had befallen their team.

Now that interstate teams are allowed into what was once the VFL, Kelly is a Crows supporter, though they can't hurt him the way Norwood could. That's always the way: a team you chose as an adult never comes with the same emotional heft as the one you supported as a kid. Still, he likes his footy a lot. In 2011 he was the coach of the Espy Rockdogs, with the Bulldogs' Bob Murphy being handpicked as assistant coach, a team of current and former musicians who play in the annual fundraising Reclink Community Cup event. It originated in Melbourne, where they play a team representing community radio station 3RRR, but has since expanded to see matches in other states. The best on ground is awarded the Steve Connolly Medal, named after the legendary guitarist in the Coloured Girls and presented by his brother, footy journalist Rohan.

Since 'Leaps and Bounds' Kelly has penned several other pieces that are inspired by Australian rules. In 2015 while he was working on a project to put some of Shakespeare's sonnets to music, he wrote one of his own and dedicated it to a new Sherrin.

In 2019 he was approached to write a song for the documentary *The Final Quarter*, about the relentless booing of Adam Goodes. Kelly wrote 'Every Day My Mother's Voice', sung as a duet with Dan Sultan. The songwriter was inspired by the way Goodes took a lesson from his mum Lisa Sansbury, a member of the Stolen Generation, on how to go forward amid such a storm of racism.

While Kelly initially felt the lyrics were 'kind of banal', they certainly struck a chord with Goodes. 'Paul is one of my favourite Australian musicians and it's a huge honour to know that he's written a song that pays tribute to my mum Lisa,' he said on social media, 'and to have Dan Sultan singing with Paul is awesome and makes it even more special for me. My mum has been such a significant influence in my life, and this song captures the spirit of our relationship and my love for her.'

Racism was also a component of another footy-related song Kelly released in 2021. 'Every Step of the Way' was inspired by hearing Eddie Betts, who played for Kelly's team the Crows, talking in an interview on *AFL 360* with Mark Robinson and Gerard Whateley about having to deal with racism over and over again: 'Eddie Betts has brought joy to me and so many others with the amazing feats he's performed on the field for 17 years,' Kelly explained to *Rolling Stone*, 'but he's shown even more class and courage off the field in talking about the deep hurt of everyday racism.'

During that interview on *AFL 360* Betts said he'd been racially abused at least once a year for the past decade. He also spoke of a world white people don't ever have to experience: 'I've got to set up barriers every day when I leave the house, thinking I'm going to get racially abused when I'm driving or when I go to a supermarket. All I want to do is rock up to training, play and enjoy the game of footy. I'm sick and tired of it, but I want the AFL to be a safe platform for young Aboriginal kids to come and enjoy and play footy without being racially abused.'

There was a phrase in that interview that Betts kept coming back to, one that created a spark of inspiration for Kelly. In that interview Betts kept returning to the point that he was sick and tired of the abuse and that he wanted to keep educating people, so Kelly chose to use the phrase 'sick and tired' in the chorus of the song.

The song also includes a line that was a reference to a 2021 incident where Betts' former Crows team-mate and captain Taylor Walker was fined and suspended for six weeks for a racial slur in an SANFL match: 'There is no excuse or justification for the words I said,' Walker stated in the statement released by the AFL. 'They are unacceptable and I take full accountability for that.'

Betts, who was playing for Carlton at the time, said an apology wasn't the end of the story: 'He needs to learn from this. He needs to own it. And he needs to work towards educating himself to be anti-racist, educating people around him, calling people out on racism when he hears it. Doing that is the only way we're all going to move forward on this.'

The former forward had a much more upbeat view of Kelly's song about him. 'I was so honoured when Paul reached out to me with a song that he had written from his heart,' Betts said to *Rolling Stone*. 'He has always empowered us mob with his music and his authentic and heartfelt collaborations have always been enjoyed by myself and all my family for many years. I feel proud to have this song written for me by someone so respected here in Australia and someone who has always stood in solidarity with us mob. This song means a lot to me.'

16

IT'S BLACK AND WHITE

It wasn't the first time Nicky Winmar had been racially abused while playing footy, it was just the first time he had chosen to let everyone know about it. It was 17 April 1993, in a round 4 clash where Winmar's Saints were up against Collingwood at the Magpies' Victoria Park. It was a decrepit venue, due to be phased out as an AFL venue before the turn of the century. In their book *Black and Proud* Matthew Klugman and Gary Osmond call the place the 'most feral real estate in all of football'. It was an oval where men urinated in beer cans rather than push their way to the toilets, and those toilets overflowed more often than not.

It was also the place where players of any skin colour other than white could expect to be subjected to some abhorrent abuse, which is what Winmar and Saints team-mate Gilbert McAdam heard as they walked out of the players' tunnel at half-time in the reserves to check out the condition of the ground. It involved comments around lynching, petrol sniffing and threats to kill, the sorts of comments that are usually said while people are safe in the anonymous embrace of a mob. McAdam remembered the anger surging when the comments started, but reined himself in. He spoke to Winmar and said they had to play a special game to make a statement.

So they did: McAdam's performance netted him three Brownlow votes and Winmar got two in the Saints' 18.18 (126) to 15.14 (104) win. Of course, the negativity from the Collingwood fans didn't respect that at all: being whipped just made them angrier, so Winmar left his celebrating team-mates and walked over to the area where the Magpies cheer squad was massed, and it was fortunate that two newspaper photographers saw that and decided to keep him in the frame of their cameras.

There is no video footage of Winmar's brave moment that day, and the only visual record are the photos taken by *The Age*'s Wayne Ludley and John Feder from the *Herald Sun*; if you've got an image of what happened in your mind it will most likely be one of the photos they took that day. Without those photos all there'd be are the words of those who witnessed it, and we know what they say about the relative value of pictures and words. Winmar looked at the Magpies fans, smiled and turned around, then he lifted up his guernsey, pointed to his skin underneath and told them: 'I'm black, and I'm proud to be black.'

Unsurprisingly, those who most needed to listen to that message ignored it and instead stoked their own anger. Winmar and his family spent the night at the home of celebrity Saints fan Molly Meldrum and it was a good thing they did, for irate Collingwood fans had left abusive letters at his house that threatened violence upon him and his family. Three days later Collingwood president Allan McAllister told the media that players copping racist abuse really wasn't a big deal, that they were all copping it and while you wished it didn't happen it was the nature of sport.

The following weekend McAllister added further flame to the fire, even knowing it was a hot-button issue: 'As long as they conduct themselves like white people off the field, everyone will admire and respect them. As long as they conduct themselves like human beings, they will be all right. That's the key.' When he justifiably copped it for those ill-thought remarks, for some reason he headed to the Northern Territory to issue an apology even though First Nations people live in Collingwood and support the Magpies.

Along with McAllister, plenty of football fans completely missed the significance of Winmar's gesture. One felt Winmar had brought the abuse upon himself by pointing to his skin, indicating that it was not the crowd's fault for being racist but the player for standing up to it. A 74-year-old Footscray fan felt racial abuse was perfectly fine and all part of going to the footy, and was comfortable with telling a *Sunday Age* journalist, 'Of course, I sing out "Black bastard", but I don't mean it. It's all part of being at the footy on a Saturday arvo. The media makes too much of it [racial taunts]. It's just a way of letting out your feelings.'

It's as simple as this: if you don't have a problem with someone's race then don't racially abuse them. Racial insults are *not* the same as any other insults, and racial abuse is against the law. As beautifully expressed by *The Age*'s Patrick Smith: 'At the very best, comments made in "the heat of the battle" trivialise what is a shameful world problem – the persecution of people because of the colour of their skin – and remains very much an Australian problem as well.'

It was certainly a Collingwood problem: in the wake of the Winmar incident it came out that Collingwood fans had an unenviable track record when it came to racism. Several players came forward to say they'd been abused while playing and one of them, Jamie Lawson with the Swans, said Collingwood supporters and players were the worst in the league: 'They call us niggers and all that,' Lawson told *The Age*'s Smith. 'Yes, it does go on. Some of the players, some of the Collingwood players, have a go at us. They call us black bastards and everything else.'

The Collingwood fans certainly didn't get the message. McAdam's brother Adrian played for North Melbourne and when the Kangaroos turned up at Vic Park he copped the same racism, but he also used it to inspire himself and kicked an impressive nine goals in an 83-point flogging. He waved to the troglodytes in the outer after Wayne Carey goaled in the last quarter.

Despite calls in the media just two days after the Winmar incident to make racial abuse a reportable offence, the league dragged its heels for more than two years. It took the public embarrassment over a 1995 incident, again involving Collingwood, for it to finally act. In the first Anzac Day clash in 1995 against Essendon, Collingwood's Damian Monkhorst racially abused Michael Long. The Bombers player, who had been silently copping abuse for years and often responded with his fists, demanded the AFL do something and they did, eventually banning racial abuse and drawing up a new rule that empowered umpires to report it. This opened the way to suspending players and fining clubs for incidents of racial abuse.

While this was definitely a move in the right direction it didn't solve the problem; the appalling treatment Adam Goodes received at a match against Collingwood is testament to that and to people's ability to avoid facing the reality of what their words and actions say about them. One Collingwood president made a King Kong joke about Goodes and then later took to the Nine Network to criticise an on-field celebratory war dance by the much-lauded Swan, because he hadn't notified people ahead of time that he planned to do it.

Racism is far from being a Collingwood problem, but the Do Better Report commissioned by the club found there was something distinct and egregious about Collingwood's history. The report also included the Winmar and Long incidents in a brief selection of racist abuse at the hands of Collingwood players and fans: '[It] gives the impression that the racism is entrenched, as though, as one interviewee commented, reflecting on the frustrations about the structural elements of racism in the Club, that "racism appears to be a part of Collingwood Football Club's DNA".'

The report's authors noted that the club had been making improvements since it was handed down in 2021 that included a formal apology in 2023 to Winmar and McAdam. 'The Collingwood Football Club understands that racism is harmful and has no place in our game and apologises to Nicky Winmar and Gilbert McAdam for the hurt they experienced playing football,' the apology read in part. 'It takes courage to stand against racism and when First Nations people do so it is our opportunity – all Australians – to listen, learn and change for the better.

'Collingwood also apologises for the appalling comments made by its most senior official in the days following that game.'

The club had got the message, although it seemed some of the Magpies fans were still a bit slow on the uptake. In 2023 Port Adelaide forward Willie Rioli was abused online after a close match against Collingwood in round 19, then four weeks later a Collingwood fan racially abused the Lions' Charlie Cameron, with a spectator in the crowd taking a photo of the fan and posting it online. At a Lions home game against Collingwood earlier in the 2023 season, Cameron was also singled out. Unfortunately, abuse happens not just among Collingwood fans but across the board. Dogs player Jamarra Ugle-Hagan copied Winmar's iconic gesture after copping racist abuse from a St Kilda fan.

It's pretty sad that more than 30 years after Winmar lifted his guernsey and pointed to his skin some people still haven't got the message.

17

THE ELEPHANT AND THE LION

Marketing people must hate footy: for them it's all about the match-day experience, about what happens before the game and during the breaks in the game and even about how to distract people *during* the game. It's all predicated on the mistaken assumption that the footy isn't enough, that if only they offered more then more people would go through the gates.

However, it's the undeniable truth that not one person in the long, storied history of Australian rules has ever bought a ticket to a match because some hack pop star will be performing their new single while standing on the back of a ute, dancers will be walking around the ground or some radio station's promo team will be giving away T-shirts people will never wear. They come for the footy, because the footy is enough; fripperies are not needed to entertain people during breaks in play. Besides, that's when most people are queuing at the toilets or the bar, so they're not even in the stands to watch whatever form of entertainment is on offer.

One possible starting point for this sad state of affairs was at Arden Street in round 5 of the 1978 season. The Kangaroos were hosting Collingwood, a grand final rematch. The two sides had played in the first drawn grand final in 1977, the same year the rugby league decider ended in a draw, and it had required a replay, in which both sides managed to score quite a bit more than the 76 they had each scored in the first match. On top of that, North was on a four-match winning streak to start the season and looking good to be there when the whips were cracking. They were playing the Magpies, who tended to drag their huge supporter base along wherever they played in the VFL.

Someone decided that wasn't enough excitement for the afternoon and that someone was former Kangaroo Barry Cheatley, who had been hired by the club as the league's first marketing manager. He came up with the idea of bringing an elephant onto the field. 'One of our pennant members was a man named Jack Allan,' Cheatley told the North Melbourne website. 'He was a bit of a character and he owned Allan Amusements. To promote his circus it was decided that we'd bring out an elephant.'

The elephant was brought out by a handler, and because that wasn't enough it was decided to get one of the cheer squad members to ride on its back. The willing volunteer was eight-year-old Sally Wood: 'I was in the cheer squad and they asked if anyone wanted to ride an elephant and being a plucky eight year old I put my hand up and said "Me, me, me",' she said in the *Herald Sun*. 'I vaguely remember it was supposed to kick footballs. I just remembered getting on it, it running amok and everyone just scattering and me hanging on.'

While the elephant could deal with the crowds under the big top, a massive horde of 31,424 punters was way more than it was used to and especially when most of the horde were Collingwood fans, who proceeded to cheer when their team ran on the field. The elephant startled and began jogging down the wing for 10 to 15 seconds, with a handler grabbing a rein or an ear and Sally Wood bouncing around on top and holding on for dear life.

The funny thing about the incident is that nothing much really happened; it's as though the incident lives on because of the potential for what could have happened. Through an incredible stroke of good luck the elephant calmed down just as it got to an open gate between the advertising hoardings, which led directly to a densely packed crowd of people. Had the elephant continued to freak out and try to escape off the field and into the crowd there could potentially have been carnage and Cheatley might have been looking for a new job, so we can watch the footage, have a bit of a laugh and perhaps breathe a sigh of relief that it could have been so much worse.

Despite the elephant incident living long in the memory, it hadn't exactly ruled a line under bringing live animals onto the field. In 2014 Brisbane Lions CEO Greg Swann plugged the idea that a live lion – albeit caged – on the turf of the Gabba would be a top idea. Perhaps the lion would serve as a distraction, momentarily making fans forget the other Lions' ordinary on-field efforts: they finished 15th in 2014 with seven wins. 'We don't know if we can get it up,' Swann told the SEN radio morning show. 'We're having a look at it. We think the kids would be absolutely beside themselves so we're just having a talk to a few zoos and lion parks about how it would work and we've had a chat to the AFL and fortunately the boss thinks it's a great idea.'

Gillon McLachlan, the boss in question, was on the same radio show a half-hour later to support the lion idea. He spoke the dreaded words 'match-day experience', saying he had been at the clubs to figure out what they could do to make a day at the footy more exciting because, you know, the footy just wasn't enough. 'Greg's taken this to another level. Whether it's realistic or not, I'm not sure . . . It's a provocative idea that's got lots of different angles and can be done sensibly.'

Not surprisingly there was strong opposition to the idea, including from RSPCA Queensland. 'If they are considering it in any form, we would be very much against it and do everything in our power to stop it,' the RSPCA's Michael Beatty told Guardian Australia. 'It would be very, very stressful for the lion and unfortunately at large events such as that, there are always idiots who will throw something or try to take the lion on. There are too many variables. We have moved on from the days of the Roman arenas, frankly.'

Someone at the Lions came to their senses and the idea was ultimately dumped.

THEY COME FOR THE FOOTY, BECAUSE THE FOOTY IS ENOUGH; FRIPPERIES ARE NOT NEEDED TO ENTERTAIN PEOPLE DURING BREAKS IN PLAY.

I THOUGHT THE ONLY WAY THIS WAS GOING TO GET THE ATTENTION OF THE AFL WAS TO CAUSE A BIT OF A RUCKUS . . .

18

THE SOUND OF SIRENS

Chris Connolly insists there was method in his apparent madness that afternoon in Launceston. At Aurora Stadium – York Park if the naming rights disgrace is jettisoned – on 30 April 2006, Connolly's Fremantle Dockers were up against St Kilda. The Western Australians were ahead by 27 points midway through the third quarter and Saints coach Grant Thomas benched the taller forward Fraser Gehrig, in part because he gave away five free kicks through various scuffles with almost half the Dockers' team, for Nick Riewoldt in preference for a smaller forward line.

It paid off: the Saints slotted seven of the next nine goals to bring the score to 14.10 (94) to 13.15 (93). After a big lead in the second half the Dockers were only a point in front, with 35 seconds to go. After the centre bounce the ball was in play for a while, then a stoppage kicked in on the Dockers' halfback line with just eight seconds on the clock. Fremantle managed to repel the Saints, locking the ball up right as the time ran out.

Or did they? Several Fremantle players believed so and raised their arms in the air in jubilation. On the match footage not a single Saints player can be seen head in hands rueing a close loss. The TV coverage cut to the Fremantle coaching box, where Connolly and everyone else were rising to their feet, stretching their legs and heading out the back door. However, down on the field the game was still going. More Fremantle players were waving their arms at the umpire, who ignored them and bounced the ball.

Then it got really confusing. Play continued for about 20 seconds and the Saints' Steven Baker kicked a wobbly old behind. Umpire Matthew Nicholls was approached by the other men in bright yellow, who appeared to be telling him the siren had sounded. About 20 seconds later Connolly made his way onto the field, barking orders at someone.

Then it got really, *really* confusing. Almost two minutes after Baker's point, during which time all the players had been milling around the umpires, he was awarded a free kick. Nicholls said Baker had been bumped by Daniel Gilmour as he kicked, and Nicholls decided that as the kick happened before the siren he would be paid a free. Baker's initial behind didn't count but his next score, also a behind, did, and St Kilda had got away with a draw. Well, for a few days anyway.

Welcome to what has become known as Sirengate. The core of all the drama was the difference between the rules and common sense, the latter saying Fremantle won by a point and the former that the game wasn't over until the umpire acknowledged the siren. Ah, what a mess. To be fair to Nicholls no siren can be heard in the television coverage, not even when you know when it was supposed to sound and crank the volume up to a level that annoys your neighbours so can you hear it. The commentators themselves didn't even hear it.

ABOVE When Bulldogs coach Luke Beveridge called up Bob Murphy after the 2016 decider to hand over his medal to the injured clubman he created an iconic grand final moment.

LEFT Luke Beveridge's selfless gesture to hand over his Jock McHale Medal to Bob Murphy was honoured with an award from the Sport Australia Hall of Fame.

RIGHT St Kilda coach Grant Thomas's dislike of some umpires' performances in 2005 paved the way for what became known as the 'Whispers in the Sky' controversy.

ABOVE With his blond hair and tight shorts there's no doubt Warwick Capper was an attention seeker, though the overexposure led to a form slump during his time with the Sydney Swans.

LEFT When a cat food manufacturer offered the struggling Geelong side cash if one of their players would change their name to 'Whiskas' for a week, Garry Hocking took one for the team.

LEFT The back of the first Brownlow Medal awarded in 1924 to Edward Greeves. Charles Brownlow, for whom the game's most prestigious individual award is named, actually once floated the idea of merging Australian rules and rugby league to create a hybrid code.

BELOW Footscray's Neil Sachse in hospital days after a collision with an opponent left him a quadriplegic in what was just his second game for the Bulldogs.

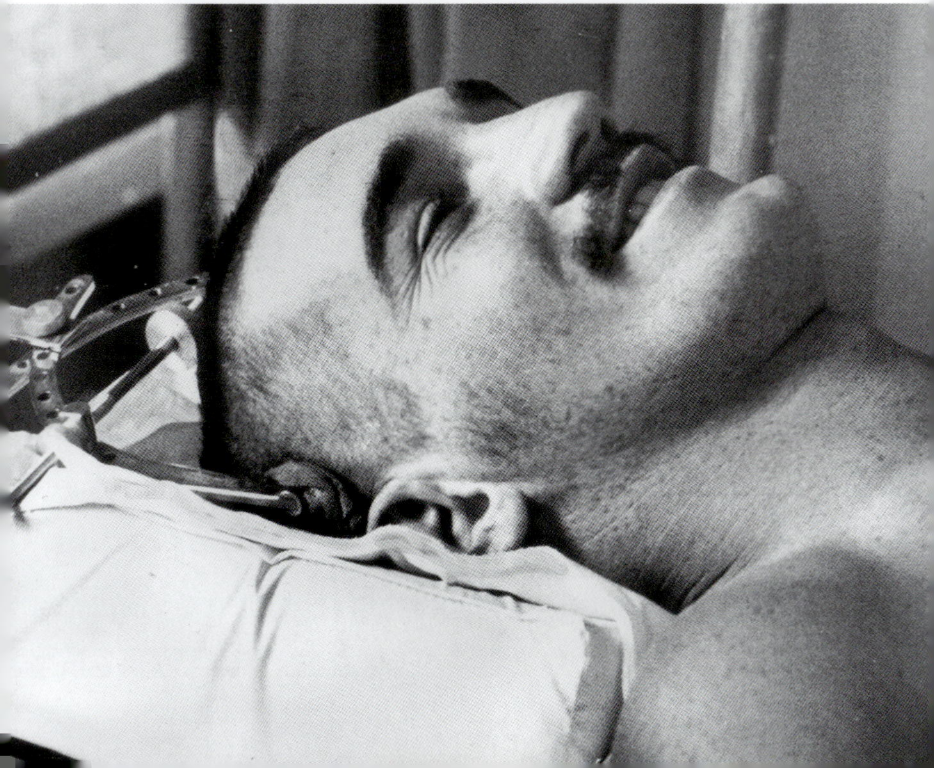

LEFT Brad Johnson takes an on-field mark against Geelong in 2002. In the 2010 season he found it hard to get on the field after being clipped by a golf cart during training.

BELOW In 2011 Meat Loaf was responsible for one of the all-time worst moments in grand final entertainment.

ABOVE Essendon's Tim Watson could win a flag, but singing defeated him. Watson was one of the players who recorded a song for the infamous *Footy Favourites* album.

LEFT Tayla Harris, who stood up to the trolls that commented on a photo of her, poses next to the statue based on that image. The statue is outside Docklands.

ABOVE After winning the big one in 2019 Richmond Tiger Jack Riewoldt managed to get onstage with The Killers, who performed after the grand final.

BELOW When looking for song-writing inspiration, Paul Kelly has turned to the footy more than once.

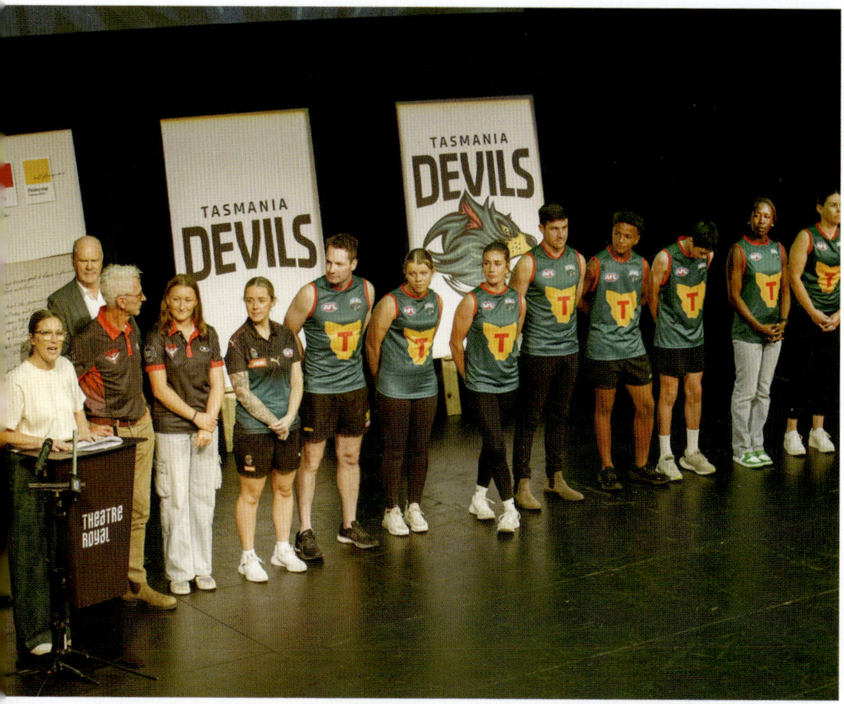

ABOVE The Tasmania Devils are the newest AFL side, due to enter the AFL in the 2028 season.

BELOW Kevin Sheedy's jubilant celebrations after a 1993 win over the West Coast Eagles, in which he took his bomber jacket and swung it over his head, was enough to inspire a rivalry.

LEFT Nicky Winmar stands up to the racist abuse from sections of the Collingwood crowd during a 1993 match.

BELOW West Coast Eagles fans were shocked when Sydney Swans' Michael O'Loughlin got in their faces after kicking a goal in 2006.

The reason why cranky Connolly marched onto the field was to create enough of a scene that the AFL couldn't sweep it all under the carpet. 'I thought the only way this was going to get the attention of the AFL was to cause a bit of a ruckus,' he told the Dockers website years later, 'so I stormed out on the ground and had it out with the umpires. It was a bit messy but it was the only way it was going to get to the forefront. We're in Tasmania, it's Fremantle, there's not much interest there from the Victorian side of things.'

What also helped was a long plane ride back home. Usually that sort of thing is horrible after a draw or a loss, but CEO Cameron Schwab saw it as a chance to get his ducks in a row before they landed and the offensive against the AFL could begin. 'The benefit was that we were getting on the plane and getting back to Perth, so we had five hours to really formulate what we were going to do next,' he told the Dockers website. 'We had all the people who were involved in it, in a confined space and available to discuss everything. I was able to interview the players, people who were sitting on the bench, who heard it or didn't.'

Schwab was able to make sense of what the hell had happened. It had been a windy day, so the sound of the siren was carried away on the breeze. To make it even more inaudible, Nicholls happened to blow his whistle for the last ball-up at the same time the siren made its feeble cry. The timekeepers thought Nicholls' whistle had been his acknowledgement that their work was done. 'It turned out the timekeepers were basically packing up until someone tapped their window from the Crown Lager box next door to tell them the game was still being played,' Schwab told the Dockers website. 'That's why there was such a delay between them blowing the siren again.'

That became their strategy: that the timekeeper was at fault because they should have kept sounding the siren until the umpire signalled he'd heard it. However, the Dockers would be nice about it as going in and spraying anger around the AFL boardroom would just get the bosses' backs up and likely see the draw stand. At the same time York Park venue manager Robert Groenwegen was trying to protect the image of the oval, and of Tasmania. 'We didn't want to be seen as a place where things went wrong,' he told Fox Sports. 'It wasn't a faulty siren although you could argue it could have been louder.'

Three days after the final siren, whenever it actually sounded, the AFL decided the Dockers had won by a point. There had been some toing and froing as the league didn't want to intervene lest it open the floodgates for umpire complaints that affected the result of the game, but after a four-hour hearing they came to the conclusion that the circumstances in the Fremantle–St Kilda match were so unusual that changing the result wouldn't set a precedent. Effectively, the blame went to the time-keeper for not continually sounding the siren until the umpires acknowledged the end of the match, even though the timekeeper *did* initially believe the umpires had done exactly that.

As commission chair Ron Evans said: 'The AFL Commission has determined that the correct interpretation of the relevant rules and regulations is that the match concluded immediately after the siren was sounded to end the match in the final quarter.

The effect of this interpretation is that Fremantle Football Club won the match.' While making the statement, Evans issued a rather rare mea culpa from the AFL: 'As the organisation charged with the management of the competition, the AFL accepts full responsibility for what took place and unreservedly apologises to the clubs involved, the players and football fans.'

It was a decision that got Connolly out of a tricky situation: he had been in a spot of bother for entering the field while a game was in progress. However, the league ruling the game was over when the siren sounded meant Connolly's cranky pitch invasion happened after full time, so therefore he wasn't on the field during the game.

The league decision marked only the second time in the code's history that a final score was overturned in a board meeting. The only other time (see Chapter 5) was a 1900 game in which St Kilda was playing, though that time the post-match ruling favoured the Saints.

. . . WHEN IT COMES TO SHORT COACHING STINTS IT’S HARD TO BEAT THREE DAYS.

19

THE SHORTEST COACHING STINT

If you want some level of job security it's best not to pursue a career as a footy coach. As long as you're winning games you're fine, but drop a few in a row and then the media speculation starts about how much longer you've got in the top job and how you need to turn things around quickly or face the sack. It's not that uncommon for a coach to be sent packing after a single season. It's also not unheard of for a club to punt a coach before the season's finished, figuring a caretaker could hardly do any worse than what the other guy had been dishing out. However, when it comes to short coaching stints it's hard to beat three days.

That's how long Bervyn (or Bervin) Woods was the coach of Collingwood. The committee appointed him the night of Thursday, 14 April 1950 and he quit a few days later, on Sunday night. Ultimately, his misfortune was to be stuck between two club legends. Woods had been coaching the twos when legendary Collingwood leader Jock McHale decided he'd had enough and announced he wouldn't be in charge of the side. McHale had coached the Pies for 38 years, starting as captain–coach in

1912 and bringing home eight flags in that time, including four straight from 1927 to 1930.

McHale was a hard, hard act to follow as it was, but Woods also had to deal with team captain and fan favourite Phonse Kyne. Most people believed Kyne was unbackable to take on the role of captain–coach, including the man himself: 'I am disappointed but the committee's decision is final and I will abide by it,' he told *The Herald* on the Friday. 'I will play in the practice game tomorrow.'

He didn't. Over the next 24 hours Kyne had a massive change of heart and decided to retire from the game. 'If I played again, after what happened, I would feel a hypocrite,' he explained to *The Sporting Globe* a few days later. 'Rather than be that I have retired as a Collingwood player.' While he wasn't suiting up to play, Kyne went to Victoria Park to watch the practice match and perhaps to wallow in the adoration of the crowd. He was mobbed by thousands of them and reportedly carried on their shoulders for about 50 metres.

The various club officials who voted for Woods (there had been rumours the club had promised him the job if McHale ever quit) didn't fare anywhere near as well: they were jeered and hooted at by Collingwood fans. *The Age* reported that one supporter tore his ticket in half and threw it in the face of a committeeman, saying 'Take it, you are ruining the best club in Australia.'

Rather unfairly, Woods also came in for some heckling. The response from fans and the somewhat petulant resignation of Kyne meant Woods was able to read the enormous writing on the wall and chose to resign for the sake of team harmony, proving his quality as a clubman at the same time. 'I feel,' Woods wrote in his resignation letter to the club, 'that I cannot accept the position of non-playing coach of Collingwood. It is quite obvious that I cannot expect the united support of all . . . I have taken this action in the hope of restoring the unity and good feeling which has always prevailed at Collingwood. Whatever decision the committee may now make, the coach appointed is assured of my loyalty and support.'

Woods effectively quit as coach without coaching a single match for points. With the season kicking off that weekend it meant the Pies were without a first-grade coach or one in the reserves either. On Tuesday night they fixed that and voted Kyne as first-grade coach and gave Woods his old job back at the twos, but Kyne played silly buggers by not saying for a day or so whether he would accept the job offer. Finally, he did what everyone knew he was going to do and said he'd take it. With that sort of lead up it wasn't a surprise Collingwood lost their round 1 match against the Swans 14.12 (96) to 11.10 (76).

If the men on the committee thought that would be the end of things they were sorely mistaken. The anger over the coaching decision was still flowing a month later when a special meeting was held at the Collingwood town hall. A vote of no confidence in the board was passed by the astonishing margin of 500 votes to 40. Kyne was there playing his part, directing his players to attend and be among those pushing for the board's resignation. In a show of poor form Kyne also decided to sling some mud at Woods via *The Argus*: 'I was prepared to play under great old stars like Syd Coventry or Harry Collier or Albert Collier, but I have no faith in Bervyn Woods as a coach – even though he is a good chap.'

Several players told the media they would have withdrawn from that Saturday's match against Geelong if the no-confidence motion had failed. With the win under their belts, Kyne was sure the players would move on. 'The fight's over, so far as the players are concerned,' he informed *The Argus*. 'We are not letting it worry us because we realise we have to concentrate on the game and I don't think the boys will be upset by what has happened.'

Well, they might have been, maybe just a bit. The Pies led at the end of each quarter and went into the three-quarter time huddle up by 27. In the final quarter Collingwood clocked off: the Cats kicked five goals to one and only ended up losing by one point.

A week after the no-confidence motion the Magpies committee all stepped down, including Harry Curtis, who had served as president since 1925. He and any other committee member deemed to have voted for Woods over Kyne wouldn't be re-elected. On the field Kyne's team wasn't going too well: with a round 10 match against St Kilda coming up and the team sitting in seventh place, Kyne decided to emerge from retirement and play in the ruck. By round 14 he'd picked himself at full forward and kicked two of the team's 17 goals in a 17.14 (116) to 12.7 (79) thumping of Carlton, but he retired again two weeks later. He continued as coach through to the 1963 season, winning two premierships in that time.

20

LIGHTING IT UP

Footy played under lights is pretty common these days; the league and the TV networks love it because they can show matches in prime time when people are at home parked on the lounge. What is surprising is that not only does night football predate the founding of the AFL in 1990, it is also older than the VFL – which played its inaugural season in 1897.

Melbourne saw its first night game in 1879, the same year Thomas Edison gave his initial display of the incandescent bulb. That match took place on 5 August at the Melbourne Cricket Ground between teams from the East Melbourne Artillery and the Collingwood Rifles. The event created such excitement that the police chose to stop all traffic near the Melbourne Cricket Ground (MCG) in the early evening to reduce the risk of accidents. It appears no one knew just how the crowd would react to a night game; there was certainly some thought that people would take advantage of the darkness to creep over the fences. To that end a large body of police would be on hand along with a detachment from the artillery unit.

Whether the game itself was any good depends on which newspaper you read. *The Age* was sold on the concept, saying 'A wonderful success had been achieved. Those who visited the ground had every reason to be satisfied. The scene was a beautiful one.' *The Argus*, on the other hand, left the ground unimpressed, noting the lights creating a very peculiar scene somewhere between a strong moonlight and twilight: 'The play did not excite much interest as the men were continually going out of sight into dark patches and the ball, though painted white, required too much of an effort for the eye to follow it.' There was also the problem that one of the five lighting rigs at the MCG blew fairly early in the match.

It's also not entirely clear who won the match. The *Bendigo Advertiser* said the Artillery team won, while *The Argus* report suggested the game ended prematurely in the second half: 'After playing a little longer the Collingwood players suspected they were opposed by more than 20 men and ceased playing to count their opponents. They stated there were 21 [A]rtillerymen, which was stoutly denied by the latter. The spectators, believing the game was over, thronged onto the ground and the match ended in some confusion.'

The first match played under lights for points happened in round 8 of 1952, during what the media dubbed the 'propaganda round'. The VFL's grand idea was to play the six games of that round outside Melbourne in a move to try to sell the game to the northern states. The weekend's matches made up an extra round on top of the normal 18 home and away matches in a bid to counter claims from supporters that they'd see just 17 rounds in Melbourne. Collingwood and Richmond travelled to the Sydney Cricket Ground, Geelong and Essendon went to Brisbane while Fitzroy and Melbourne played in

Hobart. Three other games were played in rural areas: Albury (North Melbourne versus Melbourne), Euroa (Carlton versus Hawthorn) and the Gippsland town of Yallourn (Footscray versus St Kilda).

The propaganda round idea wasn't embraced by all clubs, six of which voted in February 1952 to stop it while 17 votes were in favour of the venture. Collingwood was opposed to playing premiership matches outside Melbourne, which was the same feeling held by Geelong. St Kilda thought the whole thing was a waste of money. However, it went ahead and it was a bit crap.

The Sydney match had been heavily promoted, with posters placed around the town that read 'This is not an exhibition match. This is the real thing. This is fierce red-blooded Australian football. No quarter given or asked,' but the weather wrecked the game. 'The Collingwood–Richmond game in Sydney was probably a bad, instead of a good, advertisement for the Australian code,' *The Age* reported. 'Heavy rain, which began on Friday night, turned the Sydney Cricket Ground into a quagmire . . . [T]he teams failed not only to put on a good spectacle of the game, which was understandable in the conditions, but to give a reasonably good display of wet-weather football.' While the crowd was reported to be 24,174, many of them supposedly left halfway through to catch a nearby rugby league match with a 3.15 pm kick off.

After the game Collingwood president Syd Coventry and secretary Gordon Carlyon released a joint statement saying the match failed to sway Sydneysiders to their code: 'Collingwood opposed this match, however, we fulfilled our part of the bargain and we let our effort speak for itself,' they told *The Herald*. 'People trying to foster the game in Sydney should be helped but the Collingwood–Richmond game has not assisted them at all. People who saw the game in the mud were greatly disappointed.'

Rain also wrecked the Footscray–St Kilda match at Yallourn, but the worst of the matches was the Bombers and Cats in Brisbane – the one match of the weekend to be played under lights. The rain bucketed down from Friday and the locals didn't seem too keen on preparing the showground field. Three rugby union matches were scheduled to be played there on Saturday afternoon, before the Victorian sides took the field that night. In the end the VFL match didn't take place on Saturday night because the ground officials felt it would severely damage the playing surface. Essendon and Geelong officials were unhappy, saying they'd played on worse fields in Melbourne.

There were moves to reschedule the match for Monday night, though Geelong wasn't sure because a large number of players had to arrange extra leave from their employers. There was also the issue of accommodation: with Brisbane in peak tourist season, according to *The Sportsman*, all the hotels were booked out so some players would have to move elsewhere. If the match wasn't played one league official suggested the whole round would have to be replayed.

In the end all the players got the extra time off work and the match went ahead at 7.30 pm on Monday, but the Geelong side were not happy about it: they would have to catch a pre-dawn flight the next day to get back to Melbourne and prepare for the following weekend's match against the Swans. 'South have lost one game – they played last Saturday and are already home and rested,' Geelong secretary Ivor Gibson told *The Herald* the day before the Essendon clash. 'They will train normally tomorrow night. Geelong are still marooned in Brisbane. We are not happy about it but this propaganda match has to be played and there is nothing we can do about it. Geelong did not want to come up here and have always opposed this away from Melbourne game.'

That attitude may explain why Geelong got absolutely pasted. Bombers full forward John Coleman kicked 13 goals, one more than the entire Geelong side. The final score was 23.17 (155) to 12.14 (86). Despite being played under lights, the match reports don't even mention that.

While night footy now happens all the time, the idea of sending a round of matches to far-flung places all over the country wouldn't be repeated.

AS WARNE HIMSELF DESCRIBED IT THAT GAME AGAINST CARLTON WAS A DISASTER. IT STARTED TO GO WRONG BEFORE THE OPENING BOUNCE . . .

21

WARNIE

It's incredibly hard to make it to the top level of footy. Only around 80 players are drafted each year, about 0.3 per cent of the eligible club footballers across the country according to the AFL, and that's just to get on a club's list. Even if a player makes it that far there's no guarantee they will crack if for a single game in the seniors, and if they do it's no certainty they might avoid getting cut down the line. It really pays to have a plan B, and as far as plan Bs go it's hard to get any better than a job as a legendary Australian Test cricket spinner. Such was the fate of Shane Warne, who suited up for St Kilda in the under-19s but blew his big chance to rise up the grades.

He was making a bit of a name in the Mentone Grammar school team so the Saints came knocking. He played a few games for the under-19s while in years 11 and 12 but the school games took priority. It wasn't until he finished school that he was able to play a full season in 1988 and he did okay, kicking seven goals against his childhood team Hawthorn. As Saints' development manager John Beveridge told the St Kilda website: 'He had some ability, Warnie. He had lovely hands and he could kick it well. He was always beautifully balanced and used whatever height he had well – but we didn't know a lot about his cricket then.'

Warne's under-19s coach Darryl Nisbet added another piece of the Warne make-up: 'He had shit in him and he took it to cricket [a reference to playing with aggression].' In the team photo that season Warne stands out even though he's seated on the far right of the photo. It's not his physique that does it, though he is doing the footballer's trick of folding his arms and making fists so as to try to make his biceps stand out; it's his peroxide blond mullet. He seems quite proud of it, though he really shouldn't.

His big chance came when St Kilda was hit with injuries and a number of the reserves were called up to the AFL. That led to Warne getting the call from reserves coach Gary Colling: the peroxided one was getting a start in the twos. It wasn't great timing for Warne; in his autobiography *No Spin* he said he'd been sick with the flu all week and was just about to call the club and pull out of the weekend match when Colling called. Not knowing when or if this chance might come around again, Warne said 'Yes.'

As Warne himself described it that game against Carlton was a disaster. It started to go wrong before the opening bounce: St Kilda historian Russell Holmesby remembered he was listed in the *Football Record* as 'Trevor' Warne. On the field he was at full forward marked by defender Mil Hanna. The Carlton player was still making his way in the AFL world; having ruptured his ACL in his first senior's game in 1986, he was still working his way back up the ladder.

Colling told the 17-year-old Warne that he was expected to chase Hanna if he took off with the ball. Whether it was the flu or a full forward's natural tendency to stay in the goal square and let team-mates worry about his man, Warne didn't chase. Several times he didn't chase and each time Colling sent out a runner to get in Warne's ear, but then the coach drew a line through the kid. 'I saw [Hanna] taking three bounces, finishing the third bounce at the scoreboard,' Colling told journalist Jake Niall. 'I said "That's it – get him off."'

The game is one Hanna still gets asked about from time to time. 'I ended Shane Warne's football career,' he joked. 'I burnt him off his feet. I remember this kid with bleached blond hair, but to be honest, I didn't know who he was . . . [I]t wasn't until years later that I finally realised. Imagine what might have happened if he played well? I reckon I did the world of cricket a favour.'

That one shot in the reserves signalled the end of Warne's time with the Saints: before the start of the 1989 season he got a letter in the mail saying the club didn't want him anymore. While his dad insisted Shane was sick and shouldn't have played in the reserves match, with uncharacteristic self-reflection Warne felt it was more than that: 'The truth is that I wasn't good enough – not a mile off, but in the end not good enough,' he said in his autobiography. 'That's hard to take. It went deep, like my soul had been ripped out. I was in love with AFL football but the game was not in love with me.'

He eventually got over the break-up and played his first state cricket match for Victoria in 1991, then made his Test debut against India in January 1992. In that match he returned the appalling bowling figures of 1/150 but he got better: a lot better. While playing he held the record for most Test wickets with 708, and he only lost the record when Sri Lanka's Muttiah Muralitharan overtook Warne after his retirement.

During his cricket career Warne still kept in contact with the Saints. He had become friends with the St Kilda star Trevor Barker, so much so that when Warne returned from the Pakistan tour where he was offered money from 'John the Bookmaker', Barker was the first person he called. When he was suspended for failing a drug test after taking a diuretic his mum had given him because she felt he was looking a bit chunky, Saints coach Grant Thomas let him train with the team. Warne also served as an unpaid member of staff that year after the AFL ruled he couldn't hold an official position while serving out the drugs ban.

In 2012 he got to pull on the Saints jersey and play for the club in a Legends match played before the clash with the Greater Western Sydney Giants, and he looked in better shape than most of the other players on the field. Warne enjoyed it so much he backed up again for the 2015 Legends match.

When he died in March 2022 it hit the club hard. While he may have grown up a Hawthorn supporter, he had long become a hardcore Saints fan. In a statement published on the Saints website club president Andrew Bassat said: 'The Saints tribe has lost today one of its most passionate and committed members. As many know, Shane loved talking football and his love for the club was matched only by the quality of his insights. He put in so much – our last contact was on Sunday when I asked him, yet again, to do something to assist the club and he of course unhesitatingly agreed.'

Former Saints captain Nick Riewoldt remembered the feeling Warne engendered in new players coming to the club: 'One of the real highlights when you got drafted to St Kilda was knowing you were going to the club that Shane Warne barracked for and, hopefully, one day you were going to get to interact with him,' he told *The Sydney Morning Herald.*

The club paid tribute to Warne in its first match of the season, against Collingwood at Marvel Stadium. His kids Jackson and Brooke came out to toss the coin before the start of the match, while St Kilda's warm-up tops were emblazoned with number 23 instead of their usual numbers and both teams wore black armbands in the match. The Saints didn't win that game, but for one match something mattered more than the final score.

. . . A FOOTY GAME TAKES A FEW HOURS. IT'S NOT SUPPOSED TO TAKE A FEW DAYS . . .

22

FOOTY'S LONGEST GAME

From the opening bounce to the final result, a footy game takes a few hours. It's not supposed to take a few days, but that's what happened in the 1996 round 10 match between St Kilda and Essendon. Twenty-two minutes into the third quarter at Waverley, Essendon were up 9.9 (63) to 6.7 (43) when the ball was thrown in at the Bombers' forward pocket. As Ryan O'Connor kicked towards the sticks the floodlights flickered a few times and went out, with the stadium plunging into darkness.

While most players stood around wondering what to do next, O'Connor raced straight to the man with the flags. 'I tried to bluff the goal umpire into awarding a goal but he told me he had no idea where the ball was,' O'Connor told *The Age*. 'There was total confusion.'

That was putting it mildly. The league obviously didn't think such a thing could happen, as there was nothing in the rule book to sort this one out quickly. Essendon's Mark 'Bomber' Thompson was an electrician and he knew this was a big problem, telling club manager Danny Corcoran they were in a bit of trouble. The lights in the towers needed at least 15 minutes to cool down before the power could be switched on, though that was only if the power could first be restored.

The players milled about lost for what to do, then the runners came on the field and brought them into huddles. St Kilda coach Stan Alves spoke to them near the player's race because there was some light there, before the team moved into the sheds. That was a mistake: it was pitch black in there.

On the field the league officials were looking for a way forward. 'There is nothing in the rules of the game [that] covers this sort of circumstance,' league communications manager Tony Peek explained to *The Age*. 'We spoke about how long would be a realistic time for the players to be off the field before we could restart. Both clubs felt that 10.15 pm would be the latest we could leave it. Then it was going to take a whole lot longer to get the power back on here at the ground, so really there was no choice but to call the game off.'

Early reports said the outage was caused by a car hitting a power pole nearby, though people in the stands could see lights on in the surrounding houses. What had happened was that the fuses had blown at the Waverley substation and left scorch marks around the high-voltage switch that isolated the equipment from the power supply. When the fuses blew the switch was tripped but was too damaged to again allow the power to flow.

That was the cue for some in the stands to get the idea for a little mayhem. A few streakers livened things up before around 1,000 people stormed the ground and lit bonfires in the centre square. Down at the Wellington Road end supporters were pulling down the point posts. 'It was *Lord of the Flies*,' Bombers' captain Gary O'Donnell remembered in a retrospective published in *The Age*. 'There was anarchy. It was amazing what people do when they're in a mob mentality. Ripping goalposts, lighting them up, lighting fires, destroying things. It was a poor night in the AFL's support base.'

Essendon coach Kevin Sheedy was a little less concerned, at least about the point posts: 'They've still got to get home with a goalpost over their shoulder,' he said in that same retrospective piece. 'That'd be difficult.'

The handful of police did their best under the circumstances: a patrol car cruised the field and the police helicopter was called to offer some light. AFL boss Ross Oakley branded the ground invasion pretty disgraceful but felt police and security handled the chaos well: 'When 1,000 people invade the ground there's only one thing the security can do – stand and watch,' he told the *Sunday Age*. 'If the police or security had taken any firmer action than they did, then they could have had a riot on their hands and that would have been stupid. I thought they handled it very well.'

Oakley had to hose down concerns about what the Waverley incident meant for the AFL's plans to stage a night-time grand final: 'If you draw that long bow, you would say that we shouldn't have any night football ever again,' he chastised in *The Age*. 'Of course, that's stupid, you would never consider that. I don't think it has any impact at all.'

The big question remained: who had won the game? In fact, did *anyone* win? St Kilda president Andrew Plympton said the

Saints would be happy if both teams got 4 points but the score was recorded as 0–0 so as not to affect the percentages. Sheedy agreed they should both get the points. The league didn't agree at all: they wanted the game finished and ruled that the two teams had to return on Tuesday night and play the remaining 24 minutes in two 12-minute halves. 'In our view and in the view of the clubs and the players' association,' Oakley said in a press conference, 'it is the best option available and is the fairest option, if any of them are fair.'

Apparently no one had run this by Alves, who thought the idea was stupid and let loose on his feelings in *The Age*: 'I just think the league has taken a very weak, soft option. Their decision defies all logic. I just believe that the game was called off, finished, and they should have made a decision based on that. To go and play the remaining part of the game should never have been considered.'

Making Alves even angrier was the league ruling that any player on the teams' lists could play in the 24-minute match; whether they had taken to the field on Saturday night was irrelevant. That was a big win for the Bombers, as it meant star player James Hird, who was almost fit for the original game, could be selected. 'How can they possibly get back Hird?' Alves complained at a conference. 'We are supposed to be finishing this game off and Hird was not able to be considered for the original side.'

Almost 18,000 fans turned up for the free 24-minute match, which Essendon won 13.11 (89) to 9.13 (67) – three days after a result was supposed to be reached. While the point posts were back in place, scorch marks on the centre square turf were still visible. The AFL also updated the rule book in case this ever happened again: if a game was called off at half-time it was deemed to be a draw, and if the match was scrapped after the break whoever was in front got the point.

That rule looked like it might have to be brought into play for the 2023 round 2 Lions–Demons match at the Gabba. Brisbane was ahead by 40 points with 12 minutes to go in the match when the lights went out. Visible in one tower was a sole light still flickering, while flames sparked up inside. The floodlights were able to be powered up after 30 minutes and the match could continue, though it wasn't quite as bright as it had been before. Lions coach Chris Fagan felt the rule needed to be adjusted so that a match held up for more than half an hour should be deemed finalised and the result stand.

Fagan also felt the way the break was handled delivered an advantage to Melbourne. As he said when speaking on SEN: 'We were told to stay in the rooms and Melbourne were warming up on the ground for five minutes. 'That was an unfair advantage.' It may have helped the Demons, who kicked five goals to almost steal the match. The Lions' 40-point lead before the blackout was cut to 11 by full time.

The Gabba blackout also highlighted how urgently it needed the planned upgrade for the 2032 Olympics. 'This is probably an example of something that we hope to rectify moving forward,' Gabba manager Mark Zundans told the ABC. 'I think that this is one of the many issues that we can address through an upgrade. Ultimately, we can only deal with what we've got at the moment.'

YOU EXPECT TO HEAR OF PLAYERS PUNCHING ON, BUT AN UMPIRE?

23

ASSAULT BY UMPIRE

The 1910 season got off to a rocky start, with the round 2 match-up between Fitzroy and St Kilda making headlines for all the wrong reasons. The Lions ran out winners 14.15 (99) to 4.12 (36), but the headlines were not so much about the game but rather focused on 'football rowdyism' and 'stone throwing at Fitzroy'. *The Advertiser* reported that 'two burly navvies' gave the fans in the crowd some entertainment in the form of an impromptu brawl, then a practical joker jumped the fence and ran around pursued by several police officers before one of them managed to grab hold of him and drag him away.

The main problem was three hoodlums who were gradually rounded up in the days after the match and charged with assaulting police. The first to be pinged was Alfred Dyer, who was muscled across the ground by a number of coppers after being caught throwing stones at them. He ended up in court, where he was hit with a £5 fine. The next member of the gang to be caught was 19-year-old John Adams, who was charged with assaulting Constable Rohan and using obscene language. Rohan had been trying to arrest another man when he was hit on the back of the head by half a brick. Rohan turned and saw Adams standing a few metres away and felt sure he was the culprit, and when Adams was dragged to the lock-up he yelled out some blue words that saw him hit with an obscene language charge.

The last member to be dragged into court was Joseph Cotter, who was so drunk at the match that he couldn't remember what he did. The witnesses managed to remind him of that: he'd climbed the fence onto the field of play and Constable Rohan tried to throw him back over. Cotter didn't like that at all and whacked Rohan twice in the face. Cotter was in fact the man Rohan had been trying to arrest when Adams threw the brick at him, and Cotter was also found guilty of using obscene language. In court he was asked 'If anyone made use of such language in the presence of your sister, would you not knock him down?' Cotter could only answer that, yes, he would.

If the still-young VFL felt the season couldn't get any worse after round 2 it only had to wait two weeks, as round 4 brought a cavalcade of calamity: an umpire charged with punching a spectator, a Fitzroy player attacked as he left the field and a South Melbourne player taken to court over an assault of an opponent. The least of them was the Richmond–Fitzroy match at Punt Road. Fitzroy team-mates Clive Morrison and Edward Farrell were walking from the field when the latter heard someone in the milling crowd around them say 'Give him one.' Farrell turned just as 18-year-old Alfred Croft punched Morrison twice behind the ear. Constable Mcintosh was nearby, witnessed the attack and was quickly able to put his hands on Croft. The accused admitted punching Morrison and said he was 'so very sorry', but that didn't stop the court from fining him £5.

The next worst offence, and perhaps the strangest, was umpire and former Essendon premiership player George Hastings being charged with assault. You expect to hear of players punching on, but an umpire? The incident happened in a tight St Kilda–Melbourne clash, where the Saints went down by three points 8.6 (54) to 7.9 (51). A sore spot with the St Kilda fans was a decision Hastings made late in the match.

St Kilda forward George Morrissey was lining up for goal with Vince Coutie on the mark and Morrissey's kick landed close to the goal posts, where it was put through for a 6-pointer that put St Kilda in front, but Hastings had blown his whistle because Coutie was standing too close to Morrissey and Hastings ordered the kick be taken again. This time around there was no joy from it, so instead of winning by three points St Kilda lost by three.

The Argus criticised Hastings' decision, saying 'It was punishing them for the other side's fault to insist on the whole process being repeated. This incident caused the St Kilda followers to see all sorts of faults in Hastings' umpiring. He was certainly not a huge success but it was not bad enough to have justified the attack made upon him on his return to the pavilion.'

When the siren sounded irate St Kilda fans rushed to the members' reserved section of the Junction Oval, where Hastings would pass through a gate to his dressing room. The fans screamed out insults in Hastings' directions; *The Age* saw fit to note many of them were well dressed, as though suggesting it was usually the poorer sections of society that carried on like this.

One of the well-dressed fans punched Hastings, who decided to punch back. The only problem was that he hit the wrong person. Victor Weddell insisted he had his hands in his pockets when Hastings cracked him. A police constable on the scene refused the crowd's calls to arrest the umpire, but he advised Weddell he could press charges himself – and that's just what Weddell did. Hastings found himself on the receiving end of a summons to appear in court charged with assault. Weddell told the court Hastings had hit him twice: 'I gave the accused no provocation whatever, nor had I a stick of any kind in my hands.' There were several witnesses to the assault, one of whom said: 'The accused seemed to lose his head and hit several people who were standing around.'

In his defence Hastings said someone had thrown a handful of pebbles at his back, while he had also been pelted with sticks and stones on the way back to the sheds. 'In the passageway leading from the ground to the dressing room, he found himself wedged in by the crowd against the palings,' *The Herald* reported. 'Witness then struck out but could not say whom he hit.' However, Hastings was somehow able to insist under oath that he hadn't struck Weddell at all.

The court didn't buy Hastings' story. 'No doubt the accused lost his head and, although under police protection, he struck an offending citizen,' *The Herald* report stated. 'The accused thought that in the circumstances he was justified in fighting the crowd and that was a foolish attitude to adopt.'

Over at Princes Park, Carlton beat South Melbourne 6.13 (49) to 4.8 (32) in a match one reporter huffily said 'provided a display of ill-temper and ruffianism which thoroughly disgusted all who witnessed it'. As *The Express and Telegraph* wrote: 'Almost from the start and right up to the finish the majority of players on both sides went in for pulling, jostling and punching each other, and made no attempt to play the ball. The field umpire allowed the players to get completely beyond his control and the game became a rough, foul and unskilful scramble on both sides.'

In fairness to umpire Lardie Tulloch, another newspaper noted that if he had blown the whistle at every transgression 'the match would have been little else than a succession of free kicks'. South Melbourne's Bert Streckfuss was part of that and managed to find himself in court despite being knocked unconscious in the match. Late in the game Streckfuss gave Carlton's Andy McDonald a short elbow jolt when the pair were competing for the ball and then cocked his fists ready to go. Tulloch blew the whistle to award a free kick for the elbow. McDonald took the free, then his team-mate George Topping rushed in and walloped Streckfuss 'with a deliberate and malicious blow of the fist', laying him out cold on the Princes Park turf.

'A crowd of spectators rushed the ground and surged round the prostrate player, pushing and jostling amongst themselves,' the *Express and Telegraph* wrote. 'Two troopers rode in amongst the crowd, who surged towards the pavilion into which Streckfuss was carried in a helpless condition.'

Carlton supporters carried Topping off the field, but whether in jubilation at punching out Streckfuss' lights or to protect him from rival fans it was hard to say. Any happiness was short-lived when the league rubbed out Topping for the rest of the season *and* for the 1911 season too. 'When I interfered with Streckfuss he had struck McDonald as McDonald walked past him,' Topping had said in his defence. 'I lost my head and rushed in. I have never been cautioned before in the nine years that I have been playing.'

That good character didn't help Topping in the eyes of the investigation committee, which had had enough of this sort of behaviour: 'The mere fact of a man being loyal to his side was no justification for him to deliberately strike one of his opponents. If such things were allowed the game would fast degenerate into prize fighting.'

Streckfuss wasn't home free: after the game the commissioner of police said there was nothing to stop them from arresting a player who punched another, and that's what they did. In June Streckfuss was charged with assaulting McDonald and it went from bad to worse for Topping, for he too was charged with assault. A crowded Carlton court heard both cases, with Streckfuss the first cab off the rank. A police constable said he had seen Streckfuss hit McDonald both before and after the free kick. McDonald said Streckfuss hit him on the jaw as he went to pick up a loose ball. The umpire awarded him a free kick and Streckfuss hit him again and was going in for a third when Topping intervened. Several police witnesses who followed corroborated McDonald's story of receiving multiple punches.

In his defence Streckfuss said he accidentally hit McDonald in the jaw: 'The umpire awarded him a free kick. McDonald made a hit at me, which just grazed me. That is what made me put up my hands in self-defence. I never struck McDonald.' To highlight the unreliable nature of eye witnesses, two spectators also testified that McDonald threw the only punches.

Streckfuss was found guilty, but in terms of any punishment the court made him sweat it out until it had heard Topping's case, which immediately followed. It wasn't a long case, as Topping admitted he'd whacked Streckfuss. 'I struck Streckfuss to protect McDonald from further injury,' Topping told the court. 'I told him he was a coward as I struck him.'

Streckfuss' clear memory of events that allowed him to remember never hitting McDonald suddenly disappeared in the Topping case: 'I was standing watching McDonald going to have his kick. That is all I remember. I don't know who it was knocked me out. The next thing I remember is going home in the cab. Next day I could not stand up and got giddy. My jaw was sore for a week. It is not properly healed up yet.' For the record, Streckfuss played University the following Saturday so the injury healed pretty quickly.

Both players were found guilty and the court fined each of them £10. Streckfuss, who oddly was found guilty of assault by the court but faced no sanctions from the league, played every game of the 1910 season including the semi and prelim final before leaving to play in the VFA for the 1911 season. He never returned to the VFL, at least not as a player. In the 1920s he worked as a boundary umpire and as a goal umpire for a year in 1930.

When his league-mandated suspension ended, Topping returned to the Blues in 1912 but only played one game. He quit for the 1913 season, instead becoming an umpire, taking charge in three matches: none of which featured Carlton. After an unsuccessful stint as an umpire he returned to the Blues for the 1914 season, where he played two games before an ankle injury ruled him out for the season. Topping didn't play in 1915 but returned to the field for two matches in 1916 before retiring.

24

HEAD COUNT

When his team was up by nine points in the final quarter and it looked like there were too many players on the field, winger Norm Dare knew what to do: run. Dare was playing for West Torrens in a 1975 round 16 South Australian National Football League (SANFL) match against West Adelaide when the Adelaide captain figured their opponents had 19 men on the field, so he called for a head count. That prompted West Torrens players to run for the boundary while West Adelaide players wrestled with them to stay on the field. One of them was Dare, who managed to make it into the crowd, where he reportedly hid under a supporter's coat to avoid detection. Obviously that didn't work, because we know about it. In the end the umpires had to throw their hands in the air because it was impossible to work out just who was on the field at the time – which worked for West Torrens, who went onto win.

With the game played on such a large field there was always the possibility of an extra player sneaking onto the ground to give their team an unfair advantage, though it seems most of these transgressions are accidental. Perhaps the first documented instance of a head count was back in 1891, before the creation of the VFL. At half-time in a Fitzroy versus Essendon match several Bombers players claimed the Lions had 21 players on the field; this was back when a side was made up of 20 players. According to one report Fitzroy realised their mistake and snuck the extra player out a window at the back of the pavilion. 'It was significant that on the following Monday iron bars were placed over the window of the dressing room,' *The Argus* wrote.

In the VFL/AFL era there have only been three instances of a head count for which the match was halted and both teams lined up so the umpires could count them and none were successful, meaning the team requesting the head count was penalised. The first instance was in a 1924 St Kilda–Carlton match, where Saints captain Wels Eicke made the call. When the count was made and it was found that there were 18 players for Carlton the Saints said it was all a mistake: a player had joked to the umpire Carlton was playing with 19 men. When it was revealed Carlton had 18 on the field the player noted to the umpire 'you forgot to count yourself'.

The second instance took place in 1958 in the second-last round, between the fourth-placed Essendon and the fifth-placed North Melbourne. A top four finals berth was on the line and North was up 11.14 (80) to 7.10 (52) in the final quarter when North's big man Bryan Martin hit the ground injured. While he was being treated first-year player John Waddington raced onto the field.

Essendon officials were convinced the latter was replacing the former, who was yet to leave the field, so North had 19 men playing. Word was sent out to Essendon captain Jack Clarke to request umpire Bill Barbour count some heads, which Bombers sideline staff were sure would see the Kangaroos' score wiped: the penalty at the time for having an extra player. The game was halted, the players lined up and it was found there was no extra man. Waddington had gone on as a legal replacement for another injured player who had left the field some distance from the Essendon bench, so they hadn't seen him.

The most recent top-level head count was in 1999 when West Coast captain Guy McKenna looked around and was sure St Kilda had too many men on the field. Another attraction was that the Saints were 49 points up at the time. 'I had a quick count through the midfield, I couldn't tell that far in the forward 50 but I had a quick look at the bench,' he said on *The Front Bar*. 'Back in those days there was either two or three on the bench but someone was missing from the bench.' McKenna had to ask the umpire for a head count three times because the ump wanted know if he really wanted to go through with it. McKenna did, only to find out the Saints did have just 18 on the field.

There has been the odd head count success in lower leagues. The first was in 2013 when North Ballarat caught Frankston with 19 players on the field. Frankston had their 5.3 (38) score wiped though the players didn't realise it at the time, thinking they'd lost a nailbiter by three points when the margin was actually 41 because of the wiped score. The oversight happened because a player ran onto the field at the start of the third quarter when he was supposed to be on the interchange bench. 'It's unfortunate but Frankston have no issue with it because they know they were at fault,' said AFL Victoria state league manager

John Hook. 'Thankfully North Ballarat still won the game,' he told the AFL's website, 'so it's really a matter of percentages.'

Swans captain Brandon Jack somewhat cruelly called for a head count in a 2017 North East Australian Football League (NEAFL) match against a Greater Western Sydney hammered by injuries. Sydney was up by 100 points at the time, so the game wasn't on the line. 'Sucked the air out of the game,' Jack later posted on Twitter. 'Both teams had a bit of a laugh.'

A successful head count in a grand final is a big deal, and that's what happened in the 2018 NEAFL decider. Thirty seconds into the final term and with Southport well ahead of the Swans at 14.6 (90) to 5.5 (35), the count took place and it was found that Southport had an extra man on the field. Rather than wiping the Southport score the Swans were awarded a 50-metre free kick, because a league by-law said they could decide on a punishment other than taking a team's score back to zero.

The extra player was Josh Baxter, who coincidentally wore jersey No. 19. He'd started every quarter but had been replaced for the last term, only the grand final excitement got to him and he ran out onto the field. 'The premiership means so much to me and everyone who was there,' Baxter confessed to *The Courier Mail* after the win. 'To think I could have stuffed it up broke my heart.'

That same September weekend saw another match where a successful head count *should* have been called but wasn't. In the SANFL prelim final North Adelaide came back from a 47-point deficit to beat Woodville-West Torrens by five and book a grand final berth. However, North Adelaide had 19 players on the field for a 5-minute period of the final quarter and during that time they kicked 1.2 (8), but the extra player wasn't noticed at the time. If he had been those eight points would have been gone and Woodville-West Torrens would have been playing in the grand final a week later. Despite knowing West Adelaide had a one-player advantage for some of the match there was nothing in the SANFL rules that allowed the score to be altered after the fact. All the league could do was fine West Adelaide $10,000 and dock them four premiership points for the 2019 season.

Had the match been played under AFL rules Woodville-West Torrens would have been in the grand final. In a 2008 interchange bungle in a North Melbourne–Swans match, where Sydney kicked the match-tying behind with an extra man due to him running on the field before the player he was replacing had left it, a head count wasn't requested so the AFL's hands were tied in terms of the result. The AFL subsequently changed the rule to allow interchange officials to notify the umpire if too many players were on the field. The SANFL also changed their rules after this incident to give them the power to change a scoreline if a team had too many players on the turf.

Karma didn't have its way with West Adelaide: they went on to win the 2018 grand final, defeating Norwood 19.10 (124) to 15.15 (105).

THE NASTY STUFF CAME OUT IN THE SECOND QUARTER, WITH CHITTY BEING THE INSTIGATOR.

25

THE BLOODBATH

The 1945 grand final played between Carlton and South Melbourne just weeks after the end of World War II has gone down as the most violent decider in league history. Alongside that are questions about why that is the case, about why just weeks after the war ended such a violent match took place, but simple logic holds that one grand final has to be classed as the most violent.

If the 1945 decider hadn't been considered a punchfest then some other grand final would rise up to take the most violent mantle. Perhaps it would be the 1910 grand final, when the Magpies and the Blues went at it from before the opening bounce and Carlton back man Vic Belcher flattened Collingwood's Les Hughes before the game had started. In the final term a brawl kicked off that saw police run onto the field to intervene. Four players were suspended as a result of the all-in, two of them for 18 months.

Perhaps the most violent game was Collingwood's defeat of Essendon in the 1990 decider. The first quarter siren seemed to have been the signal for players to run in and start whacking each other: trainers, runners and even Essendon door manager John Synan ran onto the field to sort things out. The tribunal suspended four players for a cumulative total of 27 weeks along with a number of officials. Collingwood football manager Graeme Allan was out for six matches for striking Bombers' runner Peter Power. The same suspension was handed out to Collingwood team manager Eddie Hillgrove for going at Essendon boot studder Graham Menola, and Synan had to cough up $5,000 after being fined for charging at Hillgrove.

In 1985 Essendon and Hawthorn met in the decider for the third straight season. Early on both sides got into it on the wing, giving the spectators on that side of the field a good view of the action. Some players were so keen to get involved they almost ran through the umpires trying desperately to break it up.

Then there's the 1989 Hawthorn–Geelong match where Cats defender Mark Yeates ran through Dermott Brereton at the opening bounce, fracturing a few ribs. Hawks' Robert DiPierdomenico was rushed to hospital after the final siren due to a punctured lung and a few broken ribs of his own, missing the victory celebrations. Team-mate John Platten doesn't remember much of the game after playing most of it with a concussion.

If the 1945 grand final had never happened we'd likely be discussing one of the above as the most punch-happy one ever. The roughness of the 1945 big one shouldn't have come as too much of a surprise: the writing was on the wall when the fists had come out in the preliminary final a week earlier. In a match where Carlton defeated Collingwood 13.12 (90) to 12.8 (80), the rough stuff was flowing. 'Elbow jabs, sly kicks on the ankle, not-so-sly kicks in the packs and a good deal of slinging and jostling occurred for most of the game,' wrote Percy Taylor in *The Argus*.

Another report tagged it 'one of the most spiteful football matches seen in Melbourne in several years'. Both clubs pointed the finger at the other: the Carlton committee was 'incensed at the tactics of certain players' while the Collingwood secretary claimed he watched a Magpies player kicked in the face five times. Despite the reports of violence only one player was suspended, with Fred Fitzgibbon missing the grand final after copping four weeks for punching Magpies forward Len Hustler.

A much-loved story around the 1945 final has Carlton hardman Bob Chitty losing a finger in a workplace accident that morning then turning up in the sheds hours later to play in the match. No less a source than the official AFL website has relayed the story: 'Chitty wore a metal protector on the finger in the game but Collingwood's Alby Pannam accidentally stood on it and tore the plaster off,' the website said. 'Blood gushed from the finger, but Chitty refused to go off the ground and was one of Carlton's best in the win.'

As is the case with some great stories it's probably not true, partially because according to the afltables.com website Pannam didn't play in the final. It's also doubtful that Chitty even lost part of his finger before the final, although he did suffer that type of injury in the munitions plant in which he worked, but newspaper reports place that as happening in 1943 before Carlton's round 15 match-up against North Melbourne and not the 1945 prelim. On the day of the accident in 1943 Chitty didn't head to the ground with a bleeding digit straight from work either: the fingertip was lopped off on a Tuesday, five days before the game. For the 1945 preliminary final story to be true it would require Chitty to lose a second finger at work two years after the first, which just seems astonishingly careless.

After the preliminary final it was the umpires who copped the blame for the match. It really should have been the players, because if men are looking to engage in the rough stuff there's really not all that much an umpire can do, but rather than blame the grown men who did it the fault rested with the umpires.

Even *Football Record* via writer 'Substitute' laid in the boot: 'Unseemly incidents and rough play will never be stamped out whilst the umpires are so lax in their duty. The league itself has come for criticism in this matter but it's pertinent the public should know that the league itself is not wholly to blame. The umpires are appointed and virtually controlled by the umpires board, and the officials concerned will, I believe, be suitably punished for their failure to fearlessly carry out the rules.'

Substitute would have no doubt smiled when he saw that none of the umpires in the final were selected for the grand final, but head umpire in the final Alfred Sawyer apparently suffered no long-term consequences: he umpired for five more seasons, including the 1947 grand final.

Of the two combatants in the 1945 decider South Melbourne's presence surprised no one as the Bloods had been dominant all season, leading the competition for all but three rounds of the season. On the other hand, Carlton got there by grit and a stroke of luck as the Blues had started the season with three losses, prompting many to write them off. The team managed to get on track but still needed the help of the league to make the finals.

To make up for games lost during the war years the league decided to extend the season to 20 rounds. That was a huge help for Carlton, who needed all of those 20 rounds. It wasn't until the last round that they made it into the top four for the first time via a win over the third-placed Footscray, which saw the Dogs knocked out of the top four and Carlton sneaking in at fourth spot. If the league hadn't extended the 1945 season Carlton wouldn't have been playing finals footy that year.

The Blues also had the good fortune to be playing the grand final on their home ground of Princes Park, because the Melbourne Cricket Ground was still in use by the military. One might suggest the fates were aligning for Carlton. The match started at 3.00 pm, with Carlton kicking with the wind. The first quarter did nothing to contribute to the bloodbath legend, the players looking more nervous than bent on destruction. *The Age* described the early passages as 'mostly ragged, scrambling and unscientific'. Carlton was up at the first break 2.4 (16) to 0.5 (5), showing they hadn't taken advantage of the wind at their backs.

The nasty stuff came out in the second quarter, with Chitty being the instigator. While he may be looked back upon as a hard man, if he was going around today it'd be the cheap shots you'd see because that's what Chitty handed out in the second quarter. He king hit 19-year-old Ron Clegg off the ball and knocked him out, which understandably started an all-in, then he followed it with an elbow to the head of South's rover Billy Williams.

That kicked things off, with Bloods' half-back Jack 'Basher' Williams flattening Ken Hands off the ball with a punch that left the half-forward concussed and with a missing tooth and lacerated mouth. Just as with Chitty's hit on Clegg, Williams wasn't reported for that because the officials didn't see what had happened. However, Williams soon gave umpire Frank Spokes plenty to work with: immediately afterwards he shaped up against both Spokes and Carlton's Rod McLean in the inevitable mêlée that followed and also abused the umpires as he ran past them at the long break.

Williams and South didn't need to indulge in the rough stuff, as they'd kicked 40 points in the quarter to close the gap to two points at the half, down 7.5 (47) to 6.9 (45). Instead they'd gotten distracted by Chitty's brutality, which may have been the aim of the Carlton captain. Years later, in 1955, ageing South Melbourne forward Laurie Nash told *The Argus* that Chitty had gotten under their skin: 'By half-time, practically every South Melbourne player was thirsting for revenge. Our one thought while resting in the rooms was to get back on the field and settle a few scores. This played right into Carlton's hands for they suddenly gave away the man and concentrated on playing football.'

The weather helped Carlton as well with heavy rain falling through the half-time break, which worked against South Melbourne's neat passing game and in the favour of the team that showed more heart and grit.

Carlton largely forgot about the biff in the third quarter and managed to take control of the game on a muddy field, setting a 23-point lead going into the final term. Frustration seemed to get the better of South Melbourne in the last quarter, as they started focusing more on getting square than getting goals. Nash took his chance to balance the ledger for what Chitty had done to Clegg and Williams. Nash was leading out for a mark and spied Chitty set on a collision course. As the Carlton captain launched at Nash the South Melbourne forward turned slightly and clocked him. 'I put it all into that left and down he went out to the world,' Nash told *The Argus* in 1955. 'No one saw it, least of all the umpires, but Chitty's face bore the unmistakable signs for days after the match.'

It was true that the umpires had missed it: Nash wasn't reported for the punch that knocked out Chitty and sent him to the forward line where he had to lean on a point post until his head cleared. The punch kicked off another mêlée, and police had to rush onto the field to help umpire Spokes restore order. As that brawl died down another started near the boundary, with South's Ted Whitfield – who had the pre-match preparation of six beers at a pub on the way to the ground – in the thick of it. The brawl saw the unusual sight of Fitzgibbon, who had been suspended for three weeks after the preliminary final, running onto the field dressed in a navy-blue suit to take part. Again the cops intervened and took Fitzgibbon off the field.

Throughout the final quarter fists were busy, especially Whitfield's. He had been told he was being reported for trying to hit a goal umpire, so he pulled his jumper over his head and ran away to avoid having his number taken. Unsurprisingly, it was a tactic that didn't work.

Chitty ended the scoring with a goal from a free kick. Carlton had won the bloodbath 15.13 (103) to 10.15 (75), and the media went to town on the on-field chaos. 'Punching, kicking and deliberate assaults made the league grand final at Carlton on Saturday one of the worst in history,' Percy Taylor wrote in *The Argus*.

His counterpart at *The Age*, Percy Beames, felt the final quarter of the match needed little description 'except to say that rarely has a better exhibition of stadium or rough-house tactics been seen as incident after incident followed in rapid succession. All the pent-up feeling of the game seemed to be vented on opponents as big and small men charged, battered and crashed into one another violently. Elbows, fists and boots were used indiscriminately.'

As is always the case when players punch on the coverage spoke of how the public was disgusted by the spectacle, which likely misreads the feelings of footy fans, who probably revelled in the violence as they tend to do. If they didn't the bloodbath wouldn't be spoken of more than 70 years later. There was also talk about what the VFL could do to stamp out this sort of thuggery, with giving umpires the power to send off players the most popular option while another was docking a team four points if a player was suspended. Although the league pledged to consider rule changes to fix the problem, no such changes were introduced for the following season.

Immediately after the match the umpires reportedly stayed back two hours at Princes Park writing the reports that would go to the VFL tribunal the following week. When they had finished, 10 players were expected to front up and answer for their actions.

At the hearings on Thursday night the clubs were given separate waiting rooms lest things kick off again. Williams reportedly looked to get things started by sticking his head into the Carlton room to invite Chitty outside to finish what he had started, but the Carlton captain opted to stay right where he was.

The biggest suspension was handed out to a player who didn't even bother to turn up to the tribunal. Whitfield had bought a ticket to that night's South Melbourne cabaret ball, and as he didn't want to waste his money he went there instead. In his absence his charges, including shaping up to the goal umpire, abusive language and knocking the ball out of an opponent's hands after a free kick and booting it away, were heard and Whitfield was banned for the entire 18 games of the 1946 season.

Williams copped eight weeks for looking to whack an umpire and abusing a goal umpire, South Melbourne's Jim Cleary got eight for striking Hands in the final quarter and Chitty eight weeks for throwing that elbow. South Melbourne back man Don Grossman got an eight-week ban for punching forward Jim Mooring and the Blues' Ron Savage got the same punishment for whacking Grossman in retaliation.

A week later there was a separate hearing to deal with Fitzgibbon running onto the field. Because he wasn't actually a participant in the match his case had to be handled by the investigations committee. Spokes said he had seen Fitzgibbon throw a punch at an unnamed South Melbourne player but couldn't say whether it connected. In an attempt to explain himself, Fitzgibbon claimed he had seen a man jump the fence and went out to intercept him. That man was apparently stopped by a police officer but for some odd reason Fitzgibbon continued to run towards the brawl, stopping about 10 metres shy of it when he realised he shouldn't be there. The committee didn't buy it and added another four matches to the three-game suspension Fitzgibbon was already serving. That sentence took the overall tally of suspensions from the grand final to 66 weeks.

The suspensions ended the careers of five players. Outside the tribunal both Herb Matthews and Cleary were unhappy with their suspensions and announced their retirement from the VFL. Cleary, known as 'Gentleman Jim' for his on-field fairness, was upset that he would now always be remembered as one of the players suspended in the bloodbath. South's Keith

Smith was one of a few players found not guilty, in his case of striking Mooring, but he retired as well. Savage also quit as did Whitfield, who played and coached in country Victoria.

The villains in the piece, Chitty and Jack Williams, both played on in the 1946 season before retiring. That their final seasons saw them play just six and seven games respectively suggested age and not the bloodbath saw them call time.

THE LEAGUE WAS FORCED TO RE-OPEN THE INVESTIGATION AFTER A SECOND WITNESS CAME FORWARD.

26

A FEELING OF VICTORY

Ever since Watergate in the 1970s people have adopted the practice of attaching the word 'gate' to anything that is a scandal or a crisis, so some deserved kudos flow to the person who decided to call a 2015 drama 'Whispers in the Sky'. It shows a talent with words and imagery and is far better than 'Umpiregate', which some uninspired souls started calling it. Sure, nobody whispered anything and it happened on the ground and not in air, but it's still a great name.

The background to the Whispers in the Sky story started after a round 20 fixture where the Kangaroos took on St Kilda at Docklands. The Saints ran out winners 16.12 (108) to 13.7 (85) but their coach Grant Thomas wasn't pleased with the whistle-happy umpiring, and he wasn't alone: Bruce Matthews in the *Herald Sun* disparagingly referred to the match as a 'free-kick overload'. As Matthews wrote: 'This was a much anticipated third versus fifth match-up that became a stuttering affair with the whistle intervening to stop play, on average, once every two minutes.

'It wasn't a matter of whether each of the 50 free kicks was merited. They probably were. But surely 10 goals coming from free kicks is an inordinate contribution by the umpires to what was a fierce, rather than scrappy, game.'

Thomas resisted the urge to criticise the umpiring after the match, managing to wait until three days after the match, 16 August, before putting himself in line for a fine. As far as Thomas was concerned the profile of umpires was too big: 'We've put umpires on a pedestal and made them a larger part of the game than they actually need to be,' the coach told AAP. 'They should pay them whatever they need to pay them to umpire our game as mildly and quietly as they can – put their ego in the locker when they start their career and pick it up when they finish their career.'

As criticisms go it really was pretty mild. Thomas didn't suggest a hint of bias and nor did he impugn the integrity of the umpires but the AFL saw it differently, effectively showing that umpires were indeed on a pedestal and that coaches and players faced big fines if they said anything slightly less than totally praiseworthy about them. 'We certainly won't be tolerating criticism of umpires,' AFL boss Andrew Demetriou said in *The Age*. 'Our penalties are being reviewed at the moment to make them even more stringent.'

The league investigated Thomas' comments and a week later slapped him with a personal $15,000 fine and $5,000 for the club, which St Kilda decided he would have to pay himself. That the club had made him issue two separate apologies that week obviously did little to sway the investigator's mind.

Whispers in the Sky kicked off in the period between Thomas speaking his mind and then paying the price. On 19 August St

Kilda was out west, playing Fremantle at Subiaco. The home side won a tight match 12.8 (80) to 11.9 (75), and from Thomas' point of view the umpires seemed to have his comments of a few days earlier in their mind.

Before the match at Subiaco the umpires walked into the rooms as they usually do, but this time it was different. As Thomas said to SEN: 'I was leaning up against a wall with [assistant coach] Matty Rendell just talking about some match-ups and some particular strategy and the umpires walked in in single, regimented file like they do when they walk out on the ground. They walked up to the end of the change rooms, did an about-face, turned around and walked out without shaking anyone's hand or recognising anyone. It was just basically a token gesture to say "Yeah, we're here, we've been to the rooms and that's it."'

Thomas felt that meant the Saints were in for the rough end of the pineapple from the umpires but Matthew Head, the umpire at the centre of the Whispers in the Sky drama, told a very different story: the umpires had a set time to visit the Saints' change rooms but no one had been there when they arrived. 'There just wasn't . . . people around, no coaches around, no kicking balls, etcetera, so I'm not sure what happened there with the timing,' Head said on SEN.

After the match, in which the Dockers kicked five goals from free kicks – three of which were awarded by Head – he and the other umpires were boarding their red-eye flight back to Melbourne. Nine Network reporter Tony Jones had a short chat as they passed along the aisle, and what was or wasn't said became the source of the drama. Jones said he made some comment to them along the line of 'Gee, how about you blokes tonight?', to which he insisted Head replied: 'Now I know what it feels like to have a victory,' the implication being that they'd gotten one over on Thomas and the Saints.

Head insisted he said nothing at all and the umpire with him on the flight and standing next to him in the aisle, Brett Allen, backed him and insisted nothing had been said. 'My very clear recollection was that when I was getting on the plane I was standing at the start of business class walking through and . . . where I got stalled, whoever was calling the game, we were having a general conversation. You were further up the back sort of calling out to us,' Head later said to Jones on *Wide World of Sports.* 'I was having a conversation with whoever it was to my left about the game and Brett Allen said, "Don't worry about Tony," and I just continued on with the conversation and walked through.'

The league, which spent a week investigating the pedestal comments Thomas made in front of television cameras and reporters' mobile phones, somehow felt the victory accusation needed barely 24 hours to wrap up after the Nine Network reported the incident on the plane. A few phone calls were made and by Sunday night the AFL's Adrian Anderson decided it was a non-issue.

The speedy investigation didn't sit well with *The Australian*'s Patrick Smith: either Head said it and the integrity of umpires was tarnished, or he had been defamed by the Nine Network. 'It is inconceivable the ramifications of such a damning news report were buried within 24 hours,' Smith wrote. 'The Channel

Nine report went to the very impartiality of the umpires. A far more significant and damaging charge [than what Thomas said]. Yet the AFL had dismissed it by Sunday afternoon.'

The league was forced to re-open the investigation after a second witness came forward. Mitch Rentessis, a St Kilda member who was in Perth for business, was on the plane, and he said he'd also heard the comment. He thought it so significant that he chose to scrawl it down on his boarding pass.

Eddie McGuire decided to wade into the drama even though he really had no proof of anything. McGuire was boarding the same plane and said he heard the comment 'that was $20,000 and four', which he took as a reference to the $20,000 fine and the four points St Kilda gave up in the loss to Fremantle. 'I didn't know which umpire said it, or in fact if it was an umpire,' McGuire said when he called in to 3AW. 'It came from where they were standing, just as we walked past.' To sum up, Eddie heard someone say something but he didn't know who it was, so why bring it up?

On 26 August an investigation by former Victorian and Queensland assistant police commissioner Allan Roberts and ex-policeman Bill Kneebone concluded there was no evidence to support any claims of impropriety by the umpires, although Rentessis was reportedly not interviewed because he was overseas. How an investigation can be concluded without interviewing a key witness is a head scratcher.

Head spoke publicly after the finding was handed down, restating his innocence to the *Herald Sun*: 'It has been an incredibly difficult week not being able to defend myself against these serious allegations. At no point did I have any conversation with Tony Jones and the comment that is now well known in the media was definitely not made by me. This is why Brett Allen and I have asked for this investigation.'

Head umpired for three more years before retiring on 144 games, feeling that his career 'didn't keep going forward' after the incident. As for Thomas, his battle with umpires didn't stop: in 2006 he had a win when he spoke with umpires boss Jeff Gieschen following the Saints' four-point loss to Port Adelaide. The Saints had counted 14 umpiring errors, with Gieschen admitting 13 of them before being persuaded on the last one. 'I'd hate to think it was anything else other than just a bad day,' Thomas told 3AW radio. 'It was a four-point ball game, it was very tight, and we were very frustrated with a lot of things that happened.'

27

NEIL SACHSE'S LEGACY

His VFL career lasted only two matches, but Neil Sachse's legacy stretched for much longer than that. A star in the Adelaide competition, Sachse (pronounced sax-ee) was courted by Footscray for two years before signing to play for the Bulldogs for the 1975 season. He debuted against Melbourne at the Melbourne Cricket Ground, kicking his first goal in an 11-point loss.

Sachse's second and last game was at home against Fitzroy. He had been playing a blinder: his 10 marks were the best of any Doggie on the field, and he also had 14 kicks and 17 disposals. It was a good performance given how hard the ball was to control. 'It was probably because it was early in the season and the ground was hard, or maybe there was too much air in the ball, but it bounced everywhere,' he said in his biography *Playing On*. 'It was a really scrappy game because of that.'

The moment that every footy fan remembers took place in the fourth quarter, which started with Fitzroy up by 3 before Footscray slotted three quick goals. With the game clock going into time on, John Reid kicked the ball down towards

Footscray's forward pocket looking for Gary Dempsey. The ruckman was in front but couldn't grab the mark, and the ball fell behind him. A Fitzroy defender plucked the ball from the air and fired a quick handpass back to try to get things moving in the other direction.

The pass was snaffled by Sachse running through the pack. The centre half-back dropped the ball but managed to regather on the bounce. He was heading away from the Footscray goals, initially preparing to wheel around for a shot, but as soon as he got the ball under control he looked up and saw the Lions' Kevin O'Keefe, who had been running back to help out on defence, heading straight towards him.

Sachse, who began to stumble, knew there was going to be some sort of collision. He raised his right arm in the hope it would provide a degree of protection from O'Keefe's 83 kilograms, but his head speared into O'Keefe's torso and his body was bent back by the force of the Fitzroy player running past. Sachse flopped to the ground. 'He copped a real beauty,' the Seven Network commentator said.

The umpire awarded Sachse a free kick, so Peter Welsh went over and looked to slap him on the face to wake him up and take the kick. Welsh grabbed fistfuls of his team-mate's jersey and almost lifted Sachse into a seated position before realising something was very wrong: Sachse's body was completely limp and he couldn't move at all. Welsh put his team-mate back down on the turf.

Two trainers rushed onto the field, one of them wiping a towel on Sachse's face while the other was down at his feet.

Suddenly they realised something very bad had happened, and they both rose and frantically signalled for someone to bring out the stretcher. 'Not a good end to the game as far as Sachse's concerned,' the commentator said, which was a big understatement. The collision had broken his fifth cervical vertebra, damaging his spinal cord. Sachse had just become a quadriplegic.

'All I remember is going down on the ground, and I don't like getting taken off,' Sachse said in *Playing On*. When the medical staff told Sachse he wasn't going back on the field but straight to hospital, he said they'd better take off his boots first. 'We took them off a long time ago,' they told him, and that was when the reality started to hit home for Sachse.

The year of 1975 saw the introduction of colour television in Australia, which led to some teams amping up the hue of their jerseys. In this round 2 match Footscray had brightened the blue in their jerseys and were wearing red shorts, but the fact that the match was telecast had a much more lasting effect on the sport and on other sports as well. It changed the way spinal injuries are treated on the field. At the time the idea such a serious injury could happen was never in the forefront of people's minds; after all, it had never happened before but this time it was captured on television, which meant no one could ever think that again.

St John Ambulance and other groups use the footage in training videos to show what not to do. 'When I had my accident they picked me up and I said I couldn't move and they let me go again,' Sachse told *The Advertiser*. 'Now, when someone gets injured they leave them on the ground and make sure that all the protocols are in place and they take them off the ground properly. That only happens now because Channel Seven showed the game, so there was the vision of my accident.'

In a fortunate coincidence 1975 was the first year the VFL insured its players, and Sachse was the first to receive a payout under that scheme. The $180,000 he got didn't set him up for life, but it made the early years after the move back to South Australia a bit easier from a financial standpoint. After the accident Sachse made a concerted effort not to dwell on the negatives: even though he was confined to a wheelchair it didn't mean he had to spend the rest of his life in self-imposed darkness.

'It's no good blaming anybody else,' he told the ABC's *7.30 Report*. 'I had seen a lot of people when I was in hospital who seemed to want to blame everything else, even though they were part of the accident. I had a wife and two young kids at the time so I wanted to enjoy their company, so I made sure that I tried to maintain a positive attitude and get out there and do things.'

Doing things included campaigning for better disabled facilities at AFL grounds and elsewhere and setting up the Neil Sachse Foundation, which has raised millions of dollars to fund research that could help give those with spinal injuries a better life. 'People are not going to be jumping out of their wheelchairs and running off,' Sachse said in the *Sunday Mail*, 'but it may allow people to improve their muscle control, to get off respirators, to generally improve their quality of life.'

Despite only playing in two VFL matches Sachse's name is still spoken about in the footy world, especially when it comes to the gradual improvement in the rules to make the game safer.

In 2011 he spoke out against some players who were ducking into contact with the intent of winning a free kick: 'Don't duck your head,' he told *The Advertiser*. 'It's a dangerous tactic and the consequences can be a spinal cord injury. It's defeating the purpose. The AFL is trying to protect the head and the players are doing the opposite. I don't know whether it's an instinctive reaction by players to get an easy free kick. But it's definitely a dangerous practice.'

At the Bulldogs inauguration of their Hall of Fame in 2010, three pivotal moments in the club's history were recognised: the 1954 premiership, the 1989 fightback campaign and Sachse's injury. 'Sachse's courage in the months ahead and his determination over the years that followed have never been forgotten,' the cub's website states.

On 25 August 2020 Sachse passed away in Adelaide, aged 69. 'Sachse played two games for the Bulldogs after a glittering start to his career in the SANFL [South Australian National Football League], and will be remembered for the tragic injury which sadly ended his playing career,' the Bulldogs club said in a statement. 'Following the unfortunate injury, Sachse founded an organisation in 1994 to raise funds for research into the treatment of spinal cord injury.

SANFL chief executive Jake Parkinson described Sachse as 'a wonderful player who had his football career tragically cut short. However, he remained a pioneer, committed and tenacious in his pursuit for research and understanding of spinal injuries through his foundation for which our game is the benefactor. He will be deeply missed.'

An obituary on the ABC website finished on a quote from Sachse in 2016 that was a reflection of the character of the man: 'Having a positive attitude was part of my solution. By drowning in my sorrows, others around me would drown. By being happy within myself I knew that other people would follow.'

28

OUT OF TUNE

The theory that a person needed 10,000 hours of practice to be really good at anything was popularised by Malcolm Gladwell in his book *Outliers*. It has since been criticised by some for being an arbitrary figure, which of course it is, or because it suggests that anyone can succeed regardless of talent as long as they put in those required 10,000 hours.

The criticisms aren't entirely fair: Gladwell's point was that talent alone doesn't get you there. That a person needs talent and the discipline of practice to make it to the top and that just one of those two things on their own won't be enough is hardly a shocking conclusion. Does anyone really think the likes of Ablett, Barassi, Dunstall and Farmer were born to handle a ball like that? Of course they weren't; they took their latent talent and worked at it all the time: in the backyard, the street, the local park and during school footy matches.

It doesn't just apply to footy either, as the need to put in heaps of practice to be really good at something is required in every endeavour – even singing, though the efforts of various footy players might suggest some of them haven't really grasped that yet. The most obvious case in point is the cringeworthy *Footy Favourites* album, released in 1981 and featuring a representative from each of the 12 VFL teams at the time struggling their way through a song chosen for them.

It wasn't an original idea: promoter Gene Pierson had done the same thing with rugby league players in Sydney the year before and with the same title. He'd already gone to the trouble of recording the backing tracks for all the songs, so why not get a second bite of the cherry and release a VFL version?

It's highly likely that was the motivation behind the VFL album, with eight of the 12 songs recorded also featuring on the rugby league release. Both releases turn up on eBay from time to time, with the VFL version generally being priced higher than the league release. That probably says something about how heavily invested in their winter code Victorians are compared to those in New South Wales: they'll spend up to $70 on an album they *know* is going to be rubbish and it is, but as if it wouldn't be. These guys had spent their 10,000 hours kicking a footy, not holding a microphone, and singing at the end of the presentation night after a few too many beers or as part of some club hazing process doesn't make you ready to record.

Word had gone around the clubs that they wanted one player from each team to put their hand up to take part. Reportedly there was no coercion involved: all 12 participants volunteered, though some of them may have been told a few porkies to get them across the line. 'At the time we thought we were going to make some serious money, given the way they sold it to us,' Barry Round, South Melbourne's representative and Brownlow medallist, told the *Herald Sun* in 2020. 'The NRL had done the same thing and supposedly it had gone well.'

Round got lumped with Elton John's 'Little Jeannie', where the high notes were far from ideal for a rank amateur singer though he managed to get through it with the confidence booster of around a dozen cans of beer during the night-time recording session. Essendon's Tim Watson took on 'Ruby, Don't Take Your Love to Town'. He said he'd picked a country song because he felt it would be easy to sing, a mistake that's easy to make when hearing the almost conversational tone of some country and western tunes. In a radio interview years later Watson said there were more confidence boosters going around than cans of beer. He remembered a few oregano cigarettes being passed around.

Carlton's Mark Maclure, who was also persuaded with the idea the album could be a money spinner, chose 'Imagine' for similar reasons to Watson's. He thought it would be easy to sing because it had few verses and only the high note of the 'Yoo-hoo' line might pose a problem. Again, the idea of an easy song was a foolish mistake, and Maclure's effort highlights just how much effort John Lennon put in to make it sound like it was no effort at all.

Fitzroy's Laurie Serafini took on 'Hard Rock Café' and it's his version that several other performers on the album highlight as the worst. Sure, it's not good – at times it sounds as though he'd forgotten the words and stopped singing – but Serafini's song isn't the worst on the album although it certainly shouldn't have seen him with stars in his eyes. 'I had visions of *The Don Lane Show* and then a national tour, maybe even overseas,' he told the *Herald Sun*. 'I think I ended up with $360. When it came out I was a teacher in North Melbourne. The students gave me a fair bit.'

The worst of a bad bunch is Hawthorn full forward Michael Moncrieff's cover of The Police's 'Don't Stand So Close to Me'. The awfulness starts even before Moncrieff's vocals: the backing track doesn't even sound like The Police song as it was given a cheap calypso flavour that's not on the original. Then the singing kicks in – at least, that's what you assume Moncrieff felt he was doing. Really it sounds as though he's giving a spoken-word performance and is one of the few recordings on the album that needed a harmony vocal all the way through, presumably to mask Moncrieff's voice.

You'd think the *Footy Favourites* album would have shown people that singing footy players was not a good idea, but it didn't. In 1985 footy broadcaster the Seven Network decided to film a promo spot featuring players singing their jingle 'Hello Melbourne'. You can assume the call-out was for the worst singers in each club because the performances are dreadful, with some of the poor guys seeming to be reading the lyrics off a cue card. It's hard to believe no one at the Seven Network saw the finished product and said 'My god, we can't air this.'

In the late 1980s rap music joined the mainstream, and because it involved what was effectively talking rather than singing, plenty of marketing types were convinced sportspeople could do it. One of those was film and theatre composer Main Man Yuri Worontschak, who in 1988 wrote 'We Love Football', which was used as an ad for Pepsi. One player from each team was represented, with the rap giving them four lines about how great their team was before another player pushed them out of the frame and spewed out their own words. As a performance it's a definitive example of how rapping is much harder than it sounds and that white guys should tread very carefully, especially the Swans' Gerard Healy, who was such a terrible rapper that Worontschak had to dub his own voice over the top.

'Remember, this is pre-sampling,' Worontschak told the Vice website. 'There was no editing and no pitch shift, you just had to get the vocal right. And sometimes it took ages and ages but we got there in the end. It was pre-media. These footballers were just shy boys. They had no media savvy, which was good because they were quite malleable.'

Somehow, despite being quite terrible the song cracked the top 40 in Melbourne, which goes to show there was a time when attaching a VFL player to a product equated to a boost in sales.

The 1980s were the peak decade for singing footballers. Warwick Capper, who appeared in the 'We Love Football' video doing a pretty crap moonwalk across the Melbourne Cricket Ground, had an earlier go in the decade. In 1985 he released the single 'I Only Take What's Mine'. The brainwave of Swans owner Geoffrey Edelstein, the song was independently released: which means record labels saw no worth in it. Despite it being truly awful it took two people to write it, neither of whom appear to have ever written another song.

The outgoing Capper was an attention magnet so the club loaded him up with promotional duties, one of which was recording this single. It was too much for Capper to handle and led to a form slump in the 1986 season. 'The pressure took an enormous toll on Warwick,' club general manager Ron Thomas told *The Sydney Morning Herald*. 'It affected his form and it created tensions within the team. It had to be stopped before it got out of control.'

Probably the most successful song from a footy player was Mark 'Jacko' Jackson's 1985 song 'I'm an Individual', which went to number 15. Calling what Jacko was doing singing is drawing quite a long bow indeed, and judging by the accompanying music video Jacko doesn't seem to be much chop at dancing either. He spends most of his time walking towards the camera and swinging his arms like he's boxing the invisible man.

The song was written by Bob Brown, the co-writer of 'Home Among the Gum Trees', which was made famous by John Williamson. Brown also wrote the B-side of Jacko's single, 'Our Relationship is Giving Me the Creeps', which really is a song no one needs to listen to. Jackson earned the tag of one-hit wonder when his second single 'Me Brain Hurts' did nothing and went nowhere.

In 2000 Jackson and Capper teamed up to release the charmingly titled 'Rippin' Undies'. There is no sign of it online, which means either no one bought a copy or it is so bad that neither Jackson or Capper ever want people to hear it.

29

BRIBES AND THE BIG TIME

Waiting until after the opening bounce of the grand final to offer your opponent a bribe to throw the match is really leaving things a bit late, yet that's what was alleged to have happened in the 1922 VFA grand final between Footscray and Port Melbourne. The Sons of the West had been keen for an invitation to join the VFL for a few years and figured winning the VFA competition was a prerequisite for that to occur.

'It has been an open secret for many months that it was the ambition of Footscray people to see their team admitted to the league,' *The Argus* reported after the 1922 decider, 'and they regarded the premiership of the association as the principal stepping stone to that end.' Despite going on a player spending spree in which they poached players from VFL clubs Collingwood and Geelong, they went down in the 1922 decider to Port Melbourne by two points.

Footscray had made the grand final every year since 1919, which was no small feat, but Footscray had its eyes on the VFL and wanted in so badly that players and officials had allegedly tried to bribe Port Melbourne to lose the 1922 decider. Just days after the match Port Melbourne's George Ogilvie told the league the Dogs' Matthew O'Donohue offered him cash on the field several times.

According to *The Argus* report of the VFA hearings into the allegations of grand final day bribes, Ogilvie said O'Donohue approached him when he ran onto the field before the start of the grand final, saying: 'Is £20 any good to you?' After Port's fifth goal O'Donohue asked Ogilvie again if he wanted the money. At half-time Ogilvie told his team-mates what had happened, and then in the third quarter he asked O'Donohue when he would get the money. 'You will get it all right,' the Footscray player 'allegedly' replied, 'but you have got to help us win.'

In response O'Donohue denied everything and escaped any sanctions because there were no witnesses to back up Ogilvie's story, but O'Donohue wasn't the only one in the spotlight: club president George Sayer and former player Vern Banbury both had to answer claims they had attempted to bribe Port captain Gus Dobrigh along with Bill Rudd and Bill Walton in the lead up to the match.

Club secretary C.V. Sinclair told the hearings that on the day before the big one both Rudd and Dobrigh had called him to say players were being offered bribes. Sinclair himself got a call from someone claiming to be a Footscray hotel owner with a big bet on Port and who began asking all sorts of questions about the team selections, apparently with a view to removing his bet. Understandably, Sinclair felt there was something fishy going on.

There was no effort to hide identities: the two men offering the bribes met Rudd and Dobrigh in the street, so both players were able to give their names to the VFA. The Footscray club sprang to the defence of Sayer and O'Donohue, assuring supporters they were not involved. 'Statements have been made that Footscray was straining every effort to get into the league,' club secretary E. Smith said. 'This is true but the application has been made, not by the club, but by the Footscray council, which has been urging the transfer for three or four years. Such cases of attempted bribery as have been made public could do us no good.'

This brought the council's town clerk J. Gent onto the scene to defend the name of Footscray: 'We would rather lose a million premierships than gain admission to the league by such means. This year's association premiership was not necessary to secure us admission to the league. Our record for the past 10 years is good enough.'

Sayer's defence was based around the claim that he could not be at the locations Rudd and Dobrigh claimed to have met him in because for most of the day in question Sayer said he was in 'a little room in Footscray'. Despite rather suspiciously not offering any details about this little room and even refusing to answer questions about it, Sayer was cleared of any charges.

Banbury was not so lucky: despite the Footscray Hotel licensee, barman and two policemen providing an alibi by saying they saw him on the day in question he was disqualified for life, though what exactly he was disqualified from was unclear. You can assume it was from playing in the VFA, which was not a strong punishment for a man who hadn't played since 1914.

Footscray didn't get an invitation to the VFL for the 1923 season, perhaps because it wouldn't have been a good look given the bribery scandal. However, they didn't have to wait long, as the team was admitted for the 1925 season – though that, too, came to be coloured by bribery allegations.

The controversial match in question was a fundraiser between the 1924 premiers of the VFL and VFA, Essendon and Footscray, on 4 October. It became known as the 'Championship of Victoria', although the match had no official significance and almost didn't happen at all. Footscray had wrapped up the VFA crown by 20 September and had time to play the match on 4 October. However, Essendon would need to win the comp without a grand final being required because if such a match was required it would have to take place on 4 October, ruling out any Championship of Victoria contest.

The 1924 VFL season was an odd one, with the finals being a series of round-robin matches between the top four clubs. The reason for the change was to have multiple matches played on the same day, thereby spacing out the crowds rather than having them all flock to the one scheduled finals match. If the minor premiers finished on top after the round robin there would be no need for a grand final, which was the case with minor premiers Essendon. The round-robin concept was later ditched because the league realised it created dead rubbers between two sides that had no chance of winning the title, so the crowds stayed away from those matches.

With Essendon now free on 4 October the VFL–VFA clash was able to go ahead. No one gave Footscray much of a chance;

the accepted wisdom was that the VFL was the stronger, better competition, but Footscray disproved that by winning 9.10 (64) to 4.12 (36).

Essendon led by two at the half but only managed to kick 1.7 (13) across the entire second half, while Footscray booted six goals in the second half to win the match. Along with Hawthorn and North Melbourne, they were admitted to the VFL for 1925. A club made up of public service employees had also applied to join the VFL in 1925 but chose to switch to the VFA when the league took too long to make a decision, but the club's backers pulled out so the public servants never got a game in either competition. While the win over Essendon was really far from the sole factor in being chosen for the VFL, many Footscray fans were convinced it created the tipping point.

Years later the allegations flowed that Footscray had again aimed to bribe their way to a win. In a 1935 piece for *The Sporting Globe*, then Essendon player Tom Fitzmaurice insisted it was a frame-up: 'Some Essendon players were offered money to let Footscray win, and they refused it. A few others sold Essendon and the league without compunction. At the three-quarter interval a number of us expressed disgust and decided further effort was useless – we were unable to carry the dead 'uns.'

As part of his defence Fitzmaurice suggested the poor second-half performance was evidence players had been bought off. He also felt the VFL was the superior league, that on a level playing field a VFA team would never beat a VFL side.

Two days later former team-mate Charlie Hardy also spoke out, backing up Fitzmaurice's claims. As an example, Hardy offered the performance of an unnamed player when kicking to him on a lead: 'The player in possession was capable of putting the ball down my throat. Imagine my surprise to see it go skimming about 13 feet over my head . . . Before the quarter closed, I saw the same player performed the same "uncanny" feat in the same "uncanny" way on two more occasions.'

It was quite telling that none of the other Melbourne papers picked up the story, which gives a strong indication the claims were fuelled by sour grapes. It's also notable that neither Fitzmaurice nor Hardy stated they themselves were offered a bribe, and nor do they name a single player who took the cash.

Footscray club secretary C.S. Carlton understandably took issue with the accusations, responding in *The Sporting Globe* – which was clearly trying to squeeze as much out of this dubious story as it could: 'Had the players responsible for the articles any cause for complaint, it is considered by my committee that the place and time for ventilating it was not 10 years later but at the Essendon committee, immediately after the match. Maybe, however, after all these years, it is that their imaginations are running wild.'

The captain of that Footscray side, Con McCarthy, also came out and rubbished claims that Essendon were paid off, suggesting Bombers fans were looking for excuses to avoid the uncomfortable truth that a VFA side beat them.

There are plenty of factors other than Essendon players being on the take to explain the loss. Footscray won the VFA decider on 20 September and thus had two full weeks to rest and recover for the VFA–VFL clash. Essendon, on the other hand, had to play up to 27 September, giving them a week less preparation time. Also, Footscray *wasn't* a rubbish team, as they'd won the 1923 and 1924 flags and had played in every grand final since 1919. In the 1924 season they lost just one match and only two the year before, plus they had former VFL players in their ranks.

The Footscray side was allowed to use the flick pass, which was a feature of their play, while the VFL had banned the pass. Match reports make note of Footscray's hand passing, especially in the second half when they ran away with the game. Oh, and an Essendon player was a passenger for most of the match, having suffered an early injury but being forced to stay on the field because there were no replacements allowed.

Some point to the fact that Essendon smashed Footscray in their first VFL meeting in 1925, suggesting there must have been something fishy about the 1924 clash. It's true Footscray got flogged 16.15 (111) to 9.9 (63), but it's also true the Dogs were without key players rover Alex Eason, centre half-back Norman Ford and centre-half forward Jack O'Brien because they had previously transferred from the VFL to the VFA without a clearance and the league has suspended them.

As for that earlier 1922 bribery scandal? Well, it seems pretty obvious some people were looking to use their cash to help Footscray's chances of promotion to the VFL.

THE SILLY THING THE AFL DID WAS THINKING ANYONE IN AUSTRALIA REALLY WANTED TO SEE THIS HYBRID VERSION.

30

THE SHORT LIFE OF AFLX

Some ideas are just inherently stupid and should have never got off the drawing board, while others have some merit but the stupidity comes into play in the way it is implemented. The much-maligned AFLX concept was an example of the latter. The idea that the game might need some adjustments to make forays overseas is obvious: Australian rules needs big fields, which not every country has. Some overseas leagues have been forced to play on whatever vacant patches of land they can find, so looking to adjust the game to fit into a smaller rugby league/union/soccer–sized venue cancels out the size issue and increases the potential market for the sport.

The silly thing the AFL did was thinking anyone in Australia really wanted to see this hybrid version. Footy fans are super passionate and prone to argue about pretty much anything, so showing them AFLX was always going to create a frenzy of vitriol.

The AFLX concept reared its head in early 2017 with a series of trial games. The game was played on a rectangular field with 10 players a side, including reserves. Halves were

10 minutes long, and a goal kicked from outside 40 metres was worth 10 points. The league insisted that the 'X' was the Roman numeral for 10, a key number in the make-up of the new sport though almost everyone took it as another example of marketing people attaching the letter X to something in an attempt to make it seem hip and cool.

Port Adelaide chair David Koch (yes, Kochie from *Sunrise*) was an early fan, as he was already excited about pushing into China and felt AFLX would be a big help. 'It is certainly the way to take the game overseas, to play on rectangular fields, so it makes sense to do that,' Koch said in the *Herald Sun* in early 2017. 'You can't find big grass areas in China. There are lots of soccer pitches and there's a massive move in China to win the soccer World Cup in the late 2020s, so they're building all these soccer stadiums over there.'

There was a push to stage an AFLX tournament in Melbourne in the bye week before the 2017 finals. The powers that be were obviously too blinded by their own product to realise that creating a distraction the week before the peak of the AFL season – the finals – wasn't the smartest idea. Also, anyone could see a mile off that the clubs in the finals weren't going to be keen on risking players for a meaningless kick-around. 'Footy fans are being conditioned into accepting this trial smack bang in the middle of the period when the game reaches its zenith,' *The Age*'s Scott Spits wrote, 'but why divert eyes from your best product, even just for a few days?'

The players wanted to know how much they'd be paid, because AFLX wasn't in their collective bargaining agreement. Ultimately, the AFLX launch was pushed back to the 2018 preseason because it wouldn't clash with anything then – well, except for the AFL Women's (AFLW) competition that had only started the year before. So often a thorn in the AFL's side, the Western Bulldogs president Peter Gordon thought it was a stupid idea to run AFLX over the top of round 3 of the AFLW comp: 'For all of the other challenges that AFLW faces, it faces competitive product launched not from soccer or cricket but from AFL House itself,' he told *The Advertiser*. 'I'd prefer that money to go into the promotion of women's football.'

Nonetheless, the league pushed ahead and AFLX kicked off over the weekend of 15–17 February, with separate tournaments held in Adelaide, Melbourne and Sydney. While each club had to field a team, most of them saw fit to declare their key players were suffering niggling injuries that needed some rest to be right for the start of the season – or, in other words, AFLX meant nothing and there was no prize money or kudos for winning so they were not going to take it seriously. It seems the footy public didn't either. A day or two before the tournament started the AFL was slashing ticket prices and clubs were giving them away on social media.

Some in the media liked what they saw in early AFLX matches. 'The first match between Geelong and Port Adelaide showcased a product that brings frenetic non-stop action where the openness of play highlights much of what is great about our game,' the *Herald Sun*'s Jon Anderson wrote. 'Gone were the rolling mauls that have become such a blight on our code, and while facets of continuous scoring can actually become slightly boring, it's a matter of readjusting your expectations.'

Others, however, took a different view. Also at the *Herald Sun*, Jon Ralph found it to be 'footy for the Twitter generation – blink-and-miss it games over in a flash, on-ground commentators screaming at you just in case you miss a thing'. The ABC's Richard Hinds felt the best thing about the AFLX match was the final siren: 'If you wanted to kill AFL stone-dead surely you would turn it into this hollow, unappealing, pressure-free, atmosphere-deficient, oval-in-a-rectangle hole yawn-fest. AFLX is a nothing of a game. One that combines neither the best aspects of Australian rules, nor those of any other sport, but rather dilutes them so greatly that even the leather-lunged commentary box spruikers struggled to maintain their well-paid enthusiasm.'

The less said about those silver Sherrins that were ditched after the first day of games the better.

Both before, during and after the weekend of matches AFLX was most often compared with cricket's Big Bash League (BBL) with the fireworks and fast-paced razzamatazz, but it was a comparison that really didn't work. The BBL was still instantly recognisable as cricket: someone turning on the television and seeing a match knew immediately what sport was being played

The creators didn't change the size of the field or the number of players or inflate the value of a boundary to make the final scores meaningless. All the AFL had that looked like footy was the goal and behind posts. Also, the shortened form of cricket was created because the longer forms weren't attracting younger viewers. In marketing speak, the product needed a reboot; that wasn't required with Australian rules.

The three-day AFLX event drew a combined crowd of 42,730, though just over half of that was from the Melbourne matches. Around 22,500 rocked up for those matches, 10,253 at Adelaide's Hindmarsh Stadium and 9,892 at Sydney's Allianz Stadium. As you might expect, the AFL claimed those numbers were better than expected. 'We feel really positive about it,' AFLX project manager David Stevenson told *The Age*. 'When you look through the view of strong crowds, really good player feedback, good ratings, overall experience for the fans, we felt like it was a great success.'

That doesn't explain why the concept was massively changed for the 2019 series. Instead of three tournaments in three different states, it all happened on one night at Marvel Stadium. They also introduced the Gatorade Game Changer, a player who for the last five minutes of the match would have his score doubled, and a coin toss would no longer be used to decide which ends teams run to. Instead, a game of rock, paper, scissors would take place.

The club names were gone in favour of four manufactured entities called Deadlys, Bolts, Flyers and Rampage. Players were chosen via a live draft that didn't create the excitement the league might have hoped. Geelong's Patrick Dangerfield had signed on as the Bolts captain and apparently as the cheerleader of AFLX. 'To mix it up this year with different players playing with each other from different clubs is going to be well-received,' Dangerfield said in the *Geelong Advertiser*. 'The great thing about it is that there are all of these players throughout the league that you'd love to play with but you don't have the opportunity to, and this provides that platform to do it. So to have four different teams with different players from all around the country is really exciting.'

The public didn't agree: removing the clubs from the competition took away one of the few things fans recognised about AFLX. The crowd figure at Marvel was 23,828, only slightly above the Melbourne crowd of the previous year. Not even the players were fully invested, with captains telling teams to take it easy and avoid injury. 'That was a big priority of [Flyers' Nat] Fyfe and the other captains,' Flyers player Marcus Bontempelli said in the *Herald Sun*. 'To make sure we take the risk out of some of the collisions and play footy the way we know we can.'

Six months after Rampage won the AFLX flag the AFL decided the AFLX concept wouldn't return. The league finally worked out it might be an idea to focus on the competitions already running rather than looking to create new ones. As AFL football operations manager Steve Hocking said: 'There are four new clubs entering the AFLW competition for 2020, and the AFL's on-field priority next year is to ensure the right emphasis and resources are in place to ensure the women's competition continues to build on the success of the first three seasons,' he told *The Australian*. 'In addition, the AFL is assessing the full pre-season program for clubs and ways we can ensure the players and clubs are in the best condition in the lead-up to the premiership season.'

AFLX didn't go away. Instead, it became a competition for junior players, a way of introducing teens to the game – which is probably where it best fits, rather than being a concept sold to those who already follow footy.

ALL THE CLUB HAD TO DO WAS FIND A PLAYER WILLING TO LEGALLY CHANGE HIS NAME [TO WHISKAS] FOR A WEEK . . .

31

CATFIGHT

The league doesn't seem to have a problem with renaming stadiums if there's money involved, but renaming players seems to be a different story. That was the takeaway from an incident in 1999 when a pet food company paid the Geelong Cats to have captain Garry Hocking change his name to 'Whiskas' for a week.

The Cats were in a tough place both on and off the field: they were $7.5 million in debt and on a losing streak, so anyone willing to offer some money was quite welcome. Whiskas' parent company Uncle Ben's had the cash, reported to be around $100,000: with $70,000 to the club, $20,000 to the player and the remainder donated to an animal shelter. All the club had to do was find a player willing to legally change his name for a week, so loyal clubman Hocking stepped up to the plate. 'I'm probably going to cop a little bit of flak,' Hocking admitted to *The Advertiser*, 'but I see it has a great thing for the footy club and Whiskas. It's just a light-hearted thing and from a commercial point of view to help get the club out of strife.'

Geelong chief executive Brian Cook said the AFL had been approached and was totally sweet with it all: 'The AFL is sympathetic to our position and they have approved the promotion, he told *The Advertiser*. 'We got approval from the AFL for him to play under that name. We've covered all the bases. He will be registered on the team sheet, in the *AFL Record* and in Brownlow Medal voting as Whiskas.'

As expected, the footy media went through their contact books looking to get some comment from legends of the game. One of those was the Cats' own Bob Davis: 'I appreciate it as a marketing tactic, and having Whiskas play for Geelong is better than no Geelong at all,' he said in the *Herald Sun*. 'But I'm worried a marvellous career could be jeopardised by one decision. To have your captain and a four-time best-and-fairest winner in this position is a real worry, but I'd like to think Garry has done this out of loyalty to the club.'

The Tigers' Royce Hart told the *Herald Sun* he was dead set against it, saying it cheapened the club: 'Soon you will pick up a *Footy Record* and every player will have a sponsor instead of a name.' In the same article, footy legend Ron Barassi was one of the game's icons who gave it the big thumbs up: 'I think it is marvellous to see the captain of a club doing something like this to help his club and teammates.'

On the Monday before the Cats' round 12 clash against Richmond Hocking made it official, becoming known as 'Whiskas' by deed poll, then just three days before the match the AFL got cold feet despite having agreed to the deal. CEO Wayne Jackson wasn't keen on seeing the name 'Whiskas' in the *Football Record* or in the Brownlows and told the league's legal advisers to work out whether they actually had to do that. 'Obviously we would prefer not to,' he said in *The Age*. 'In future we will actively discourage such practices. It is not appropriate. We want to know if this can happen. We want to know if it is lawful to change your name one week and then another. We simply don't know. Can he change his name back again later in the year?'

These are all good questions, but it might have been better to find out the answers before the league gave Geelong its blessing. The legal advice came back that the AFL didn't have to put the Whiskas name in print, so it wouldn't. 'We have certainly decided that we will call him Garry Hocking, both from the umpire's viewpoint and the *Footy Record* viewpoint,' Jackson told *The Age*. 'We would not want to, next week, be confronted with somebody that wanted to call themselves General Motors or Fish and Chips or whatever you want to do, because I think it does have the potential to bring the game into disrepute.'

In response, Cook told *The Age* the club wasn't going to push the issue even though the league had given assurances the name would appear in the *Football Record* and the Brownlows: 'It is not a matter of life or death. We have pushed the boundaries of creative marketing within the AFL and have caused debate . . . The AFL have now had time to rethink the ramifications.'

None of this mattered to Uncle Ben's, which had been watching their product's name being mentioned all over the place. By the end of the week it was estimated the exposure was worth up to $4 million to the pet-food maker.

It didn't work out quite so well for Geelong or for Hocking: the captain was injured in the third quarter of the Whiskas match and had to leave the field, only playing two more matches in the

1999 season. The Cats lost to the Tigers by 35 points, their seventh defeat in a row. The losing streak would stretch to nine before the Cats broke it with a round 15 win over Collingwood, so the moral of the story is that changing your captain's name may bring cash but it won't necessarily bring victory.

32

THAT'S SHOW BUSINESS

The worst job in footy isn't umpiring, it's organising the grand final entertainment. A quick glance at social media on the big day shows plenty of people gleefully lambasting whichever poor soul had put the whole thing together. People have grown to expect grand final entertainment to be rubbish, so shifting that perception is hard work.

One bad grand final moment can be described in a single word: Batmobile. On grand final day in 1991 Angry Anderson hitched a ride out onto the Melbourne Cricket Ground (MCG) turf in a weird blue car. Despite it looking more like a speedboat with big bat-like wings at the back and nothing like the real thing, it was those wings that saw it tagged the 'Batmobile'.

Riding shotgun with Angry was marathon runner Robert de Castella. Deeks was there because he was the director of the Australian Institute of Sport, and Anderson because he was an ambassador of the Paralympics. The hook was that the 1992 Olympics were coming up and it was hoped Australia was bound for glory (that's a bit of foreshadowing right there). Also lined up on the turf was an array of cars carrying famous athletes and retiring footy stars whose main role seemed to be to look around and wonder what the hell was happening.

Deeks stood up in the not-really-a-Batmobile and gave a speech largely read off palm cards before handing the mic to Angry to launch into 'Bound for Glory'. As Deeks remembered in the *Herald Sun*: 'I was a bit stunned because I had no idea we were going to get in the Batmobile. Angry was pretty sedate until he got the microphone in his hand, then all hell broke loose.'

Not in the best way either. It didn't start off well: before he even got to the chorus the television cameras had switched to show a pair of athletes in one of the cars laughing out loud. Angry jumped out of the Batmobile then walked around the MCG while continuing to sing, which is never conducive to a good performance. Nor is being a tiny singer, as Angry is, alone in the massive MCG trying to entertain a crowd that didn't buy their tickets to see him.

However, Angry's performance was nowhere near as bad as some have made out. Put Angry on a stage with a backing band and have him sing the same song and, years later, no one would remember it. Angry admitted the performance was in part fuelled by rum, as someone had given him a few nips to fortify him against the cold, but the problem with the performance wasn't the booze. 'I wasn't pissed or anything,' Angry told the *Herald Sun*. 'Don't get me wrong, but it was an interesting experience because I wasn't prepared for the situation. Once you started the car, you couldn't hear over it. The sound of the exhaust was coming up through the floor of the car. It was a hard enough task trying to keep up with the track and there was a hell of an echo that went up through the stands and I was hearing myself come back in echo form.'

The reason the entertainment at the 1991 decider sticks in people's heads wasn't because of Angry's efforts, it was that damned car. It was built on the cheap by the people behind the Moomba floats because the AFL didn't have a lot of cash to splash around. However, the AFL didn't own the converted Valiant so after the grand final the Batmobile was going to be repurposed with skulls and other trinkets for various festivals, and it even reportedly showed up at a union-backed asbestos protest in the early 1990s.

In 2004 television's Kath and Kim performed at the grand final with the help of a Batmobile but it wasn't *the* Batmobile. The AFL couldn't find the original so a replica was made. That there were two Batmobiles out there would muddy the waters in the mid-2000s when one of them surfaced. A car collector named Michael Monaghan found one in a Port Melbourne tow yard and picked it up for a reported $7,000. He restored it but found the uses for a Batmobile weren't as plentiful as he might have hoped, so it sat there taking up space. He eventually decided to offload it on eBay, where it eventually went for a tick over $25,000.

Soon the new consortium of owners was concerned about whether they had bought the original or the replica. They tracked down someone involved in the making of the replica, who told them there was one surefire way to find out if they'd bought the fake Batmobile: hit it with a hammer. The replica wasn't especially sturdy and would have easily fallen to pieces.

While it's unclear whether a hammer was actually wielded, the buyers were then confident they'd purchased the original. What happened to the replica is a bit of a mystery to this day.

One performance can't blame any props for making it memorable in the worst way. Meat Loaf's terrible show at the 2011 Collingwood–Geelong decider was all his own doing. Sure, the AFL's odd idea to stick the stage in one of the gaps in the grandstand was curious, as it meant the bulk of the stadium couldn't see him, but that was minor compared with Mr Loaf's own singing. He mumbled, sang off-key and moved the mic away from his mouth to try to fake vocal effects he could no longer do. It wasn't really a laughable performance, but rather a sad one from a singer past his prime and not ready to go quietly.

Meat Loaf hadn't been in the best of health: before heading to Australia he'd fainted twice onstage in the US. As is the nature of men when it comes to their health he tried to downplay it as nothing to worry about. 'They blow it so far out of proportion,' he told *The Advertiser*. 'You faint onstage, probably that's a story. The story to me is not that I fainted onstage, the story is that I got up and finished the show.'

It turned out things were far more serious than Meat Loaf let on according to Australian promoter Harley Medcalf, who spoke after the singer died in 2022. Medcalf spent some time with a clearly unwell Loaf before the grand final show: 'He had a fever, he had the shakes, he was coughing up all the stuff from his lungs,' Medcalf said in an interview with *Today*. 'He should not have gone onstage. If I could roll back that moment, I would have grabbed him and walked him out the door, but he was under so much pressure. It rained, there was no sound check, no gear check, nothing. He was literally just tossed out there. But he was this big Texan strongman [who said] "I can do this."'

Of course, there have been good, even great, examples of grand final entertainment. One of these is the 2017 appearance of The Killers, which showed that it doesn't always have to be rubbish and, also, that sometimes an overseas act can work. The Las Vegas band played a short set before the match and another in darkness after the full-time siren. They were a band who'd had enough hits to fill out the pre-match performance, meaning even those who had no knowledge of The Killers would have heard the tunes somewhere.

Also, the band looked genuinely happy to be there, rather than having an aura of 'I'm here for the pay cheque' attitude some international grand final performers put across. They were smart enough to perform a cover of an Australian band, Midnight Oil's 'Forgotten Years', which certainly endeared them to the crowd. Who cared that lead singer Brandon Flowers kept looking down as though he was reading the lyrics from a teleprompter? The band still went the extra mile.

Richmond was in the grand final that day and Tigers forward Jack Riewoldt was a fan of The Killers, so much so that he cribbed one of their song titles for his autobiography *The Bright Side*. Risking putting a huge jinx on his team's chances, before the match he got the club's media staff to put the feelers out about the band letting him onstage for the post-match gig. Obviously, that would only be if the Tigers won: seeing Riewoldt on stage having a great time after losing the grand final would be a very, very bad look. They won, and sometime after the game as Riewoldt said in his autobiography *The Bright Side* he found himself on the side of the stage. 'Suddenly a roadie was in front of me with an instruction: "Walk up the stairs. They know your name. They might pass you a mic, but just have the time of your life."'

Flowers welcomed Riewoldt onstage for 'Mr Brightside'. As Riewoldt said in his autobiography: 'During the first few bars of the song, he sang while I danced around like an idiot. Then he gave me a mic. I was a rockstar, apparently.'

On the night of the performance Riewoldt admitted he had been a little reluctant to get on the stage, but he was glad he did. 'It [singing with the band] was close to the feeling of the final siren, the feeling of elation,' he told *The Age*. 'I can remember trying to hold the microphone far enough away from my mouth so you couldn't hear me singing, my voice was ruined by then.'

The footage clearly shows Riewoldt holding the microphone some distance from his mouth and it's impossible to hear any of his singing, though that's more likely because the road crew turned off Riewoldt's microphone before handing it over – which was probably for the best.

33

THE NAME GAME

Today, footy teams all have an official mascot or emblem. For the older sides, their mascot was often a nickname given by the barracking spectators in the crowd or the newspapers only to have the club later adopt it. The newer teams conducted contests and polls where fans were given a choice of what they wanted their team to be called, though that was no guarantee the club would listen. Sometimes the names would change over the years, because as time marched on the clubs realised they no longer worked. Here's how each club ended up with their current team name.

Adelaide Crows: the South Australian side wanted to be known as the Sharks, but the name was unavailable due to copyright issues. They then decided on the Rams, while other American team names Giants and Falcons were also considered. When the AFL knocked back Rams the board chose the Crows, possibly because of South Australians being known as crow eaters.

Brisbane Lions: this side is a combination of the Fitzroy Lions and Brisbane Bears after the former went into administration in 1996; mergers with Footscray and North Melbourne had also been floated in previous seasons. The Fitzroy side gets the prize for one of the best mascots ever. In the early years they were known as the Maroons due to the colour of their jerseys, but in the late 1930s the club decided they needed something tougher – and so entered the awesomely named Fitzroy Gorillas. In a head-scratching decision, although one that may have been prompted by rival supporters making fun of the name, club officials decided it needed an animal that was really scary so Fitzroy lost the Gorillas tag to become the much less fun Lions.

The Brisbane Bears' story is nowhere near as good. When they entered the VFL in 1987 their emblem was a koala, which many, many, *many* people have pointed out isn't actually a bear at all. 'Our Brisbane bear will be cuddly when it suits and angry when it is necessary,' the club said in a media release, convincing no one. As soon as they took over Fitzroy's AFL licence they very quickly jettisoned the Bear for the Lion, which perhaps suggests they also thought little of the koala.

Carlton Blues: the Carlton club has probably the oldest name in the AFL, with it stemming from a change to navy blue jerseys in 1871 or 1875; reports differ. While they've long been known as the Blues the name Bluebaggers, sometimes shortened to Baggers, had been a colloquial nickname for a time.

Collingwood Magpies: some match reports of the early 1900s refer to Collingwood as the 'Woodsmen', derived from the last four words of the suburb's name, but the black and white colours the club has long sported meant the Magpies name was a no-brainer.

Essendon Bombers: Essendon was one of the seven clubs to move away from the VFA to start up the VFL in 1897. Given that predates the invention of manned flight by six years, the club obviously wasn't known as the Bombers back then. They started out being known as the Same Olds before someone chose the odd option of abbreviating the back half of their name, and so they became the Dons.

There is an urban legend that says that due to the club's black jersey with its diagonal red slash looking similar to the Swans' white with the same slash the South's nickname was also appropriated. The Swans were the Blood-stained Angels, so the legend has it that Essendon were the Blood-stained N word. However, there doesn't appear to be any contemporary news reports that use that name, and not due to a reluctance to print the N word as papers of the early 1900s had no qualms about using that word.

The Bomber name came into being during World War II because of the home ground's proximity to Essendon Airport, where Beaufort Bombers were built and repaired. In 2023 the club carried out some ill-advised market research to find out if a wartime logo was still the best way to represent Essendon. Unsurprisingly, the idea of even considering changing the name was not greeted warmly by fans. In a letter to fans posted on the Bombers' website, club president Dave Barham tried to hose down the controversy: 'There is no immediate action to change the club logo or any elements of the club brand. We will always be called the Bombers.' This raised the question: what the hell was the market research about, then?

Fremantle Dockers: the second Western Australian side to enter the AFL, the Dockers joined the comp in 1994. The name the Dockers reflected Fremantle's history as a port city but it was also the source of a long-running legal dispute with Levi Strauss, which made a brand of pants called Dockers. As part of an agreement the club couldn't officially be referred to as the Dockers but Fremantle Dockers was okay, as was Fremantle and Freo, but not the word 'Dockers' on its own. You'd have thought Levi Strauss would have loved the free advertising for their pants that people had already stopped buying by this stage. Eventually the pants maker relented and the Dockers name was free to be used.

Geelong Cats: when it comes to club names, Geelong was once saddled with one of the worst. Initially called the Seagulls by the fans, some bright spark decided they should be known by the truly awful name of the Pivotonians. It apparently was a reference to the city being a pivot point for the state's rail and shipping. By 1923 a better option surfaced: legend has it that a black cat followed the team onto the ground and they played well. A *Herald* cartoonist by the name of Sam Wells played up the black cat story, suggesting the mascot could give them good luck – and so it did, so from there the name Cats gradually became synonymous with the club.

Gold Coast Suns: the Suns was nobody's first choice as a team name – well, no one except seemingly the AFL. Queensland team the Southport Sharks was involved in the bid for a Gold Coast AFL club, and the AFL said 'Yes' to their money but 'No' to the Sharks name. The league then ruled out the Dolphins and the Pirates, which had polled highly with AFL fans, and when the name went out to a public vote and the public liked the Marlins or the Stingrays the league said 'No'. It seemed the league had already picked a name: the

Suns. In a less than inspiring attempt to promote the name in 2010, club chair John Witheriff said on the Suns' website: 'The sun is bold, it's fresh, it's dependable and it's relentless. It can also be fierce and uncompromising – what other AFL teams will learn to respect about the Gold Coast Suns.' Nope, not buying it.

Greater Western Sydney Giants: these days there is little romanticism in team names, with no chance for them to evolve organically. Instead, they need a name from day one, and that opens the door to market research – which so often gets it all wrong.

Entering the AFL in the 2012 season, there was a six-month campaign to work out GWS' name that which included online feedback and newspaper polls. They were left with more than 20,000 suggestions, though presumably they weren't all different names. The options, which included Rangers, Pioneers, Stallions and Wolves, went before focus groups to decide the winner. As club CEO Dale Holmes said on the AFL New South Wales website: 'We realised that if we wanted to capture the hearts and minds of the people of Greater Western Sydney we needed to have a bold and ambitious name.' Nevertheless, they went with the bland, American-sounding name of Giants.

Hawthorn Hawks: from the Victorian Football Association years Hawthorn was known by the not very scary at all name Mayblooms. The origins of the name are in dispute, but one suggestion is that it stems from the alternate name for the hawthorn bush with its yellow fruit and brown foliage: it is also known as the May bush and its flowers are called Mayblooms.

It prompted the joke among rival fans that the club, like the flowers on the bush, bloomed in May but faded as the year wore on. In 1943 the club opted for the much tougher moniker of the Hawks at the behest of coach Roy Cazaly.

Melbourne Demons: initially known variously as the Invincible Whites and the Redlegs, the Demons soon became known by the definitely not fear-inducing name of the Fuchsias. This was because their jersey colours apparently resembled that of the fuchsia bush, although they actually don't. It wasn't until Frank Hughes signed on as coach in 1933 that the Demons tag came to the fore. According to the story he blasted the players during a break in play, telling them that they were playing like a lot of flowers and to lift their heads and play like demons. For a short period in the late 1930s they were also known as the Red Demons, before the colour reference was dropped.

North Melbourne Kangaroos: the unofficial nickname for the club was long the Shinboners, either a reference to the butchers and abattoirs in the area or the players' liking of kicking opponents in the shins. The Kangaroo tag was formally adopted for the 1950 season, though the tough nature implied by the Shinboners name saw it return in recent years. In the 1920s the club was briefly known as the Blue Birds, but they understandably ditched that pretty quickly.

Port Adelaide Power: in the South Australian competition the Port Adelaide side were known as the Magpies. When the top side moved into the AFL for the 1997 season the Magpie name was already taken, so something new was needed. Names such as Black Diamonds, Pirates, Sharks and Mariners were bandied about. Club president Greg Boulton said in 1997 that they didn't want another animal mascot but rather 'we wanted it to reflect our on-field, hard-hitting desire'. Power it was, and it had the neat alliterative option of calling the team Port Power.

Richmond Tigers: the name of the Tigers had been around the club for ages, back to the late 1800s, when they adopted a black and yellow–striped jersey that resembled the animal. The jersey colours also gave birth to the nickname the Wasps, and while it didn't last long it was better than the other name they had been called: the Richmonites. The Tiger name was effectively locked in thanks to a supporter in 1918 who couldn't afford the price of a ticket and apparently climbed a tree outside Punt Road Oval to watch. During the game he cheered them on, saying 'Eat 'em alive, Tigers!'

St Kilda Saints: due to the suburb's closeness to the water St Kilda spent an early stint as the Seagulls. In 1945 they joined the line to adopt a scary mascot and became the Panthers, but throughout the club's existence they were known as the Saints, a name that outlasted all the others.

Sydney Swans: the Swans were originally based in South Melbourne but the board had concerns about its future, so in 1982 they packed up and moved to Sydney, taking their colours and mascot with them. Due to the red and white colours on their jersey the club became known as the Bloods and the Blood-stained Angels; it's possible the latter was shortened to the former. The Swan story is that in 1933 journalist Hec de Lacy jokingly referred to the side as the Swans because of the number of Western Australian recruits;

the swan is a symbol of Western Australia. While it's hard to find any newspaper report confirming that, the club has adopted it as part of its history.

Tasmania Devils: the obvious choice for the Tasmanian side was the Devils, though Swifts and Penguins were reportedly in the mix, but Warner Bros and their copyright of the Tasmanian Devil cartoon character stood in the way. 'When it got to the point of them understanding the Tasmanian devil was actually a real animal, things freed up,' chair Grant O'Brien told InDaily. 'They understood why we were so keen to have our own animal represent the team.'

West Coast Eagles: founded in 1986, the Eagle nickname refers to the wedge-tailed eagle: the largest bird of prey in Australia, which has been known to attack kangaroos. The story goes that the nickname was chosen because as a side based on the western side of the country there would be a lot of flying involved to matches.

Western Bulldogs: while playing in the Victorian Football Association the western club was known as the Scray (the club was originally known as Footscray) or the Tricolours. There were also some more colourful names floating around in the early years: Saltwater Lads, Men from the Land of Boulders and Representatives of Stoneapolis. By the time the club joined the VFL the Bulldogs name was already there. According to legend, in 1920 club president David Mitchell was presented with a red, white and blue flag with 'Bulldog tenacity' written on it, which was potentially a link to the British Bulldog given the club colours were the same as the Union Jack. Two years later a bulldog was being stamped on members' tickets, and in 1928 the team came onto the field with the first of many bulldogs that have served as the team's mascot.

In late 1996 the club dropped the Footscray name and rebranded itself as the Western Bulldogs to market themselves to all of Melbourne's western suburbs.

PUTTING IN THE BOOT HAS LONG BEEN A TRADITION WHEN IT COMES TO THE COVERAGE OF AUSTRALIAN RULES.

BIBLIOGRAPHY

Books

Allen, Robert, *Cazaly: The Legend*, The Slattery Media Group, 2017

Cartledge, Elliot, *Footy's Glory Days: The greatest era of the greatest game*, Hardie Grant Books, 2013

Cartledge, Elliot, *Footy's Revolution: The inside story of the AFL*, Hardie Grant Books, 2018

Coventry, James, *Footballistics: How the data analytics revolution is uncovering footy's hidden truths*, ABC Books, 2018

Coventry, James, *Time and Space: Footy tactics that shaped Australian rules – and the players and coaches who mastered them*, ABC Books, 2015

Creswell, Toby, *The History of Australia in 100 Objects*, Viking Penguin, 2016

de Moore, Greg, *Tom Wills: His spectacular rise and tragic fall*, Allen & Unwin, 2008

Flanagan, Martin, *A Wink from the Universe: The inside story of the AFL's greatest fairytale, the Bulldogs' 2016 premiership*, Viking Penguin, 2018

Flanagan, Martin, *The Last Quarter: a trilogy*, One Day Hill, 2008

Hardy, Matthew, *Saturday Afternoon Fever: a footy fan's memoir of life on the outer looking in*, HarperCollins, 1999

Holmesby, Russell and Jim Main, *Encyclopedia of AFL Footballers: Every AFL/VFL player since 1897*, BAS Publishing, 2014

Hutchinson, Garrie, *From the Outer: Watching football in the 80s*, McPhee Gribble, 1984

Hutchinson, Garrie, and Ross, John (eds), *The Clubs: The complete history of every club in the AFL/VFL*, Ken Finn Books, 1998

Jarvis, Nathan, *Origin of the Speccies: The players & positions of AFL*, Fremantle Arts Centre Press, 2006

Joel, Tony and Mathew Turner, *On the Take: The 1910 scandal that changed Australian football forever*, The Slattery Media Group, 2020

Kelly, Paul, *How to Make Gravy*, Penguin, 2010

Klugman, Matthew and Gary Osmond, *Black and Proud: The story of an iconic AFL photo*, NewSouth, 2013

Lalor, Peter, *Barassi: The Biography*, Allen & Unwin, 2010

Lane, Samantha, *Roar: The stories behind AFLW – a movement bigger than sport*, Random House, 2018

Lenkić, Brunette and Rob Hess, *Play On!: The hidden history of women's Australian rules football*, Echo Publishing, 2016

Linnell, Garry, *Football Ltd: The inside story of the AFL*, Pan Macmillan Australia, 1995

Main, Jim, *Football's Black Book: Reports, charges, penalties, statistics*, The Five Mile Press, 1998

Main, Jim (ed.), *The Armchair Footy Record: For planes, trains and favourite rooms*, Geoff Slattery Publishing, 2005

Marshall, Konrad, *Stronger & Bolder: Inside the 2018 AFL final series with Richmond*, Hardie Grant Books, 2019

Marshall, Konrad, *The Hard Way: The story of Richmond's 13th premiership*, Hardie Grant Books, 2020

Megalogenis, George, *The Football Solution: How Richmond's premiership can save Australia*, Viking Penguin, 2018

Mueller, Andrew, *Carn: The game, and the country that plays it*, HarperSports AU, 2019

Murphy, Bob, *Leather Soul: The half-back flanker's rhythm and blues*, Nero, 2019

Murphy, Bob, *Murphy's Lore: Tales from the west*, Nero, 2015

Nicholson, Matthew, Bob Stewart, Greg de Moore and Rob Hess, *Australia's Game: The history of Australian football*, Hardie Grant Books, 2022

O'Reily, Titus, *A Thoroughly Unhelpful History of Australian Sport*, Michael Joseph, 2017

Pascoe, Robert, *The Winter Game: The complete history of Australian football*, Reed Books, 1995

Powers, John, *The Coach: a Season with Ron Barassi*, 4th edition, Slattery Media Group, 2017

Riewoldt, Jack, *The Bright Side,* Simon & Schuster, 2023

Ross, John (ed.), *100 Years of Australian Football 1897–1996*, Viking, 1996

Sexton, Michael and Neil Sachse, *Playing On: The incredible story of a top recruit who suffered the worst injury in footy ever, and still found the strength to thrive and inspire*, Affirm Press, 2015

Skene, Patrick, *Celestial Footy: The story of Chinese heritage Australian rules*, Hardie Grant Books, 2023

Warne, Shane and Mark Nicholas, *No Spin*, Random House Australia, 2018

Warner, Dave, *Footy's Hall of Shame*, Fremantle Arts Centre Press, 1996

Warner, Michael, *The Boys' Club: Power, Politics and the AFL*, Hachette Australia, 2022

Webber, Matthew, *The Bad Boys of Footy: Modern failings of football's finest*, Random House Australia, 2012

Wilson, Tony, *1989: The great grand final*, Hardie Grant Books, 2020

Zurbo, Matt, *Champions All: a history of AFL/VFL football in the players' own words*, Echo Publishing, 2016

Newspapers and magazines

The Advertiser (Adelaide)

AFL Record

The Age (Melbourne)

The Argus (Melbourne)

The Australasian (Melbourne)

The Australian

Ballarat Star

Barrier Miner (Broken Hill)

Bendigo Advertiser

Daily Post (Hobart)

Cairns Post

The Canberra Times
Central Queensland Herald
Corryong Courier and Walwa District News (Victoria)
The Courier Mail
Daily Herald (Adelaide)
Daily Mercury (Mackay)
Daily Mirror (Sydney)
Daily News (Perth)
Daily Post (Hobart)
Daily Telegraph (Launceston)
Daily Telegraph (Sydney)
The Examiner (Launceston)
Evening News (Sydney)
Express and Telegraph (Adelaide)
The Football Record
Geelong Advertiser
Hamilton Spectator
The Herald (Melbourne)
Herald Sun (Melbourne)
Huon Times (Franklin, Tasmania)
The Leader (Melbourne)
MX Melbourne
Newcastle Sun
North Western Advocate (Tasmania)
The Referee (Sydney)
The Register (Adelaide)
Rolling Stone
Sporting Globe (Melbourne)
Sportsman (Melbourne)
The Sun (Sydney)
Sunday Age
Sunday Mail (Brisbane)
Sunday Times (Perth)
Sunshine Advocate
Sunshine Coast Sunday
The Sydney Morning Herald
Tasmanian News
The Truth (Brisbane)

Websites

afl.com.au
afltables.com
fremantlefc.com.au
foxsports.com.au
theguardian.com.au
westernbulldogs.com.au

THE DRAMA OF THE DECIDER DIDN'T END WITH THE FULL-TIME SIREN.

ABOUT THE AUTHOR

Glen Humphries spent a decade playing fullback and back pocket for the Port Kembla Blacks reserve grade side. In that time he acquired a flag, two concussions, several broken fingers and a bunch of stitches. He has written numerous books, mainly on the holy trinity of beer, music and footy. His other Gelding Street books include *Sticky Wickets*, *Jack Gibson's Fur Coat* and *Aussie Rock Anthems.* A journalist for three decades, Glen lives and works in Wollongong.